The Financial Troubleshooter:

Spotting and Solving Financial Problems in Your Company

Jae K. Shim, Ph.D.
California State University, Long Beach
Delta Consulting Company

THOMSON

Australia · Canada · Mexico · Singapore · Spain · United Kingdom · United States

The Financial Troubleshooter
Jae K. Shim, Ph.D.

COPYRIGHT © 2005 by Texere, an imprint of Thomson/South-Western, a part of The Thomson Corporation. Thomson and the Star logo are trademarks used herein under license.

Composed by: Chip Butzko, Encouragement Press LLC

Printed in the United States of America by R.R. Donnelley, Crawfordsville
1 2 3 4 5 08 07 06 05
This book is printed on acid-free paper.

ISBN: 0-324-20648-8

Library of Congress Cataloging in Publication Number is available. See page 257 for details.

For more information about our products, contact us at:

Thomson Learning Academic Resource Center
1-800-423-0563

Thomson Higher Education
5191 Natorp Boulevard
Mason, Ohio 45040
USA

Table of Contents

About the Author

Dr. Jae K. Shim is one of the most prolific accounting and finance experts in the world. He is professor of accounting and finance at California State University, Long Beach and CEO of Delta Consulting Company, a financial consulting and training firm. Dr. Shim received his M.B.A. and Ph.D. degrees from the University of California at Berkeley (Haas School of Business). He has been a consultant to both commercial and nonprofit organizations for over 30 years.

Dr. Shim has written over 50 college texts and professional books, including *2005 U.S Master Finance Guide, Barron's Accounting Handbook, Barron's Dictionary of Accounting Terms, GAAP 2006, Dictionary of Personal Finance, Investment Sourcebook, Dictionary of Real Estate, Dictionary of Economics, Dictionary of International Investment Terms, Encyclopedic Dictionary of Accounting and Finance, Corporate Controller's Handbook of Financial Management, The Vest-Pocket CPA, The Vest-Pocket CFO,* and the best-selling *Vest-Pocket MBA.* Seventeen of his publications have been translated into such foreign languages as Spanish, Chinese, Russian, Italian, Japanese, and Korean. Dr. Shim's books have been published by Prentice-Hall, McGraw-Hill, Barron's, CCH, South-Western, Aspen, St. Lucie, John Wiley, American Management Association (Amacom), and the American Institute of CPAs (AICPA).

Dr. Shim has been frequently quoted by the *Los Angeles Times, Orange County Register, Business Start-ups, Personal Finance, Money Radio*, and other media. He has also published numerous articles in professional and academic journals. He was the recipient of the "Credit Research Foundation Award" for one of his articles on cash flow forecasting and financial modeling.

Preface

A manager's success depends largely on her ability to manage the company's assets. This mission is complicated by the way a company's finances are interwoven. One short-term financial problem, such as a cash flow shortage, can cause a longer-term credit problem, such as denial of a bank loans. The successful manager must be able to quickly identify and resolve such short-term problems to prevent those long-term deleterious effects. *The Financial Troubleshooter* is an indispensable desk reference for effective management. Covering every facet of day-to-day financial management, it is designed to help managers prevent or pinpoint and resolve emerging financial problems. In each case it presents, it also points out potential spillover effects — how a problem in one sector can disrupt operations in other areas.

Inspired in part by the practical troubleshooting books written for car and home repair, *The Financial Troubleshooter* is a hands-on, action-oriented manual for business managers, accountants, marketing managers, financial managers and officers, credit managers, entrepreneurs — in fact, for all business professionals who have fiscal responsibilities. One of the book's strongest features is its user-friendly format. Financial problem are illuminated in the following step-by-step fashion:

1. Problem.
2. Symptoms.
3. Causes.

4. Analysis.
5. Repair.
6. Prevention techniques.
7. Spillover effects.

Spillover effects, the final item covered under each problem, will be of particular value to managers who want to prevent costly systemic disruptions. Cross references throughout the book provide a running index of related areas.

Chapter 1
Cash Flow Disruptions

Failure to keep track of money may cause a business to fail. By not monitoring its cash—measuring it, investing it, borrowing it, and collecting it—an otherwise profitable operation can erode into insolvency. Without proper cash flow, a company cannot pay its bills on time, which may injure its credit rating. Bankruptcies are caused by lack of cash as well as by inability to earn a profit.

Having "enough" cash means having what's needed ready *at the right time*. Poor cash flow can cause loss of attractive opportunities, such as the ability to buy inventory at bargain prices or to pay vendors early to earn a discount. Businesses need adequate cash flow to purchase merchandise for resale, meet operating expenses, and pay debt. A situation in which a company must advise a lender, a creditor, or the Internal Revenue Service that it cannot pay indicates a lack of managerial competence. It is important to find ways to accelerate cash inflows and delay cash outflows.

The problems discussed in this chapter are:
- Inadequate cash position.
- Surplus funds.
- Delayed customer payments.
- Paying cash too soon.
- Cash outflows exceeding cash inflows.

1

- Going broke while maintaining profits.
- Inefficient use of cash.

PROBLEM
INADEQUATE CASH POSITION
SYMPTOM

Cash is unavailable to pay operating expenses as they arise—to buy inventory, to pay debt, to meet dividends, or to support expansion policies. A portion of the cash may be restricted (for example, a compensating balance does not represent "free" cash).

CAUSES

The firm's day-to-day operations are imperfectly synchronized.
- Contractual obligations require that the firm retain a minimal balance at all times.
- The company is required to hold cash balances to compensate banks for services provided.
- Weak collection policies leave the firm showing a net income but lacking liquid funds. (You *can* go broke while making a profit.)
- Cash is unavailable because it is held in a politically unstable foreign country, in a time deposit, or in a temporary escrow account.

ANALYSIS

Managers must determine what percentage of the cash balance is unavailable for use. Liquidity is improved when earnings are backed up by cash. A declining flow of cash from operations into net income indicates a cash flow problem. Look at:
- Cash flow generated from operations before interest expense.
- Cash flow generated from operations less cash payments required to pay debt principal, dividends, and capital expenditures.
- Cash reinvestment ratio (cash employed/cash obtained). Cash employed equals increase in gross plant and equipment plus increase in net working capital. Cash obtained equals income after tax plus depreciation. A high cash reinvestment ratio indicates that more cash is being used in the business.

Examine the trend in the ratio of sales to cash. A high turnover rate points to cash inadequacy. Financial problems may arise if further financing is not available at reasonable rates.

The manager must compute the following ratios:

- Cash from sales to total sales. A high ratio means that sales are generating cash flow. It also indicates quality sales dollars.
- Cash debt coverage—cash flow from operations less dividends divided by total debt. Cash flow from operations less dividends is referred to as retained operating cash flow. This calculation indicates the number of years current cash flows will be needed to pay debt. A high ratio shows that the company can repay its debt.
- Cash flow from operations less dividends divided by the current maturities of long-term debt. This ratio can be adjusted further by adding to the denominator current liabilities or other fixed commitments, such as lease obligations.
- Cash dividend coverage—cash flow from operations divided by total dividends. This ratio reflects the company's ability to meet current dividend obligations from operating cash flow.
- Capital acquisitions ratio—cash flow from operations less dividends divided by cash paid for acquisitions. This ratio reveals the company's ability to finance capital expenditures from internal sources.
- Net cash flows for investing activities divided by net cash flows from financing activities compares the total funds needed for investment (purchase of fixed assets and investments in securities) to funds generated from financing (debt and equity).
- Net cash flows for investing divided by net cash flows from operating and financing activities. This compares the funds needed for investment to the funds obtained from financing and operations.
- Cash return on assets—cash flow from operations before interest and taxes divided by total assets. A higher ratio indicates a greater cash return on assets employed. However, this ratio contains no provision for replacing assets or for future commitments.
- Cash flow from operations divided by total debt plus stockholders' equity. This indicates the internal generation of cash available to creditors and investors.

- Return earned by stockholders—cash flow from operations divided by stockholders' equity.

REPAIR

- Shore up finances immediately either by incurring debt or by issuing preferred or common shares to bring in the cash needed to operate effectively.
- Establish open lines of credit (or try to refinance if rates have fallen).
- Sell assets to generate cash.
- Enter into sale-leaseback arrangements.
- Postpone cash payments where possible.
- Rent rather than buy.
- Make only those cash payments necessary to maintain current operations.
- Reduce selling prices on products to generate cash flow.

PREVENTION TECHNIQUES

- Check the credit standings of new customers with TRW and Dun & Bradstreet.
- Analyze cash collection and disbursement processes, since these areas can be exploited to manage cash holdings more effectively.
- Analyze customer payment history, such as average number of days beyond term. Send past due notices and make phone calls promptly.

Policies should be designed to take advantage of float in the payment and disbursement system. To speed cash collections, customers should be instructed to send their payments to the company's headquarters or a nearby collection center to minimize mail delay. Customers can also be instructed to mail payments to a post office box only a few hundred miles away. The box should be emptied several times a day. Large checks, for example, those over $1 million should be picked up by courier rather than having customers mail them. Customers who make the same purchases every month can give the seller a preauthorized check (PAC) that allows the seller to write a check on the payor's account and deposit it at an agreed time. This procedure will eliminate the mail float. Companies should pay bills on time, not after but also not before they are due. Set up checking accounts in areas located a long distance from suppliers. This will increase the time it takes for a check to clear the banking system for eventual payment. For a seller large incoming cash payments can be made by wire transfer or through an automated clearinghouse to give faster access to the cash proceeds.

- Improve credit and collection policies. Encourage cash sales. For credit sales insist on a significant down payment and short payment terms. Charge interest on delinquent balances.
- Extend the maturity dates on debt to retain cash longer.
- Prepare cash forecasts to improve financial planning. The forecasts will help you be prepared for problem times when the cash position will be weak.
- Engage in joint ventures where the other company provides the cash funding.

SPILLOVER EFFECTS

If financing is available, a deficient cash position will mean you pay higher interest on loans and creditors will place restrictions on the business. A company that is out of cash cannot operate effectively. The result is declines in liquidity, profitability, and growth, and possible insolvency and bankruptcy.

See also in this chapter: CASH OUTFLOWS EXCEEDING CASH INFLOWS, DELAYED CUSTOMER PAYMENTS, GOING BROKE WHILE-MAINTAINING PROFITS, INEFFICIENT USE OF CASH, *and* PAYING CASH TOO SOON.

PROBLEM
SURPLUS FUNDS
SYMPTOM

Funds in the cash account are increasing while current liabilities remain relatively unchanged.

CAUSE

Cash generated from operations, investments, and financing is not being reinvested.

ANALYSIS

Short-term liquidity ratios can be used to determine whether surplus funds are excessive and nonproductive. Cash flow from operations to current liabilities is an effective ratio for measuring surplus funds. A ratio that keeps increasing can indicate that cash inflows need to be invested. However, cash from investments and financing should also be taken into account.

REPAIR

Companies often accumulate cash they do not need for current needs or operations. This surplus cash can be invested in marketplace securities or used to reduce outstanding debt or increase compensating balances at banks. When investing excess funds, firms must weigh the safety of the security against its liquidity, maturity, and yield. A survey of cash managers from the Fortune 1000 list of large industrial firms found that Eurodollar CDs, commercial paper, domestic CDs, and repurchase agreements were the most popular vehicles for their short-term investing. Aggressive cash managers ranked yield first, security second, and maturity third. More conservative (moderate) managers ranked security above yield, with maturity still third.

PREVENTION TECHNIQUES

- Use surplus funds to enhance earnings.
- Formulate a formal investment policy detailing sources of surplus funds, types of eligible investments, parameters of investment size and duration, executives authorized to make investment decisions, transaction reporting requirements, and parties with whom transactions can be made.
- Pay down debt regularly from operating profits.

SPILLOVER EFFECTS

Having too much cash on hand can mean lost opportunities to earn a financial return. A company that does not use its cash efficiently can eventually expect problems with financing, reduced growth, and lower profits.

See also in this chapter: INEFFICIENT USE OF CASH.

PROBLEM
DELAYED CUSTOMER PAYMENTS

SYMPTOMS

- Inability to collect an unusually large number of accounts receivable.
- Customers paying later than usual and not in full.

CAUSES

- Clients are experiencing declining profitability and depressed economic conditions.
- The company's credit department is inexperienced and ineffective.

ANALYSIS

The longer the collection period on an account receivable, the higher the company's receivables investment and the higher its cost of extending credit to customers. The bad-debt ratio, which is the portion of accounts receivables that is never collected, is one general measure of the potential for debts to go bad. The higher the ratio, the greater the cost of extending credit.

REPAIR

- Offer cash discounts to customers for early payment. This will speed up the collection of accounts receivable and thus reduce the company's receivables investment and associated costs. Offsetting these savings is the cost of the discounts that are taken, so implement a discount policy only if the return on funds obtained from early collection is greater than the cost of the discount.
- Reduce the delay in receiving customer payments by:

- Sending notices or letters requesting payment of the past-due amount.
- Telephoning or visiting the customer.
- Employing a collection agency.
- Taking legal action.

- Refuse to make new shipments until all past-due receivables are paid.
- Send coded return envelopes or custom preaddressed stamped envelopes with invoices.
- Send bills to customers when the order is shipped. The sooner a bill is received, the faster it will be paid.
- Correct invoice errors immediately. A customer will not pay a bill until it is correct.
- Require deposits on large or custom orders, or require and bill for progress payments as the work progresses.
- Set up a system to handle seasonal peak loads to avoid invoicing delays.
- Use COD terms for marginal customers.
- Charge interest on accounts receivable that are past due. If the customer has a financial problem, ask for a postdated check.
- Have customers use electronic funds transfer (EFT). With EFT, a fund transfer is credited to your bank account the same day it is charged to the customer's account. As a result, the payment float disappears, because funds are instantly available. Because it is a paperless transaction, fewer receipts are lost or stolen.
- Use customer credit cards, which are automatically validated at the retail store.

PREVENTION TECHNIQUES

To enjoy the benefits of expeditious check clearance at low cost, institute a lockbox system. Under this system, regional collection offices (such as a post of flee box or private mail box) are set up. Customers are asked to send their checks to the box in their geographic region, where a local bank picks up the checks for immediate deposit. The receiving bank remits to the company a list of checks received by account, a daily total, and any remittance documents. A returned-check document in the form of a paper or card readable by an optical character recognition device gives the business earlier notification of bad checks.

Before choosing this option, the corporation should determine the average dollar amount of checks received, the cost of clerical operations eliminated, and the interest earned because of the reduction in mail float days. Because per-item processing cost is usually significant, a lockbox is most advantageous for low-volume, high-dollar collections, but as technological advances lower the cost, the system is becoming increasingly available to small businesses with high-volume low-dollar receipts.

Cash may also come in faster if customers have given the company permission to automatically charge their accounts. This is referred to as a preauthorized debit (PAD). PADs save a company the costs of processing invoices and payments. They work well for repeated consistent charges at regular time intervals.

Lastly, through the use of debit cards at an automatic teller machine (ATM), funds may be transferred electronically from the customer's account to the account of the small business.

SPILLOVER EFFECTS

A delay in receiving customer payments may create a cash flow problem because the company is not receiving the funds it needs to go on operating. Because the firm also loses a return on the delayed cash since it cannot invest the money, profitability will be adversely affected. In the extreme case, if the company does not receive needed cash, it may risk insolvency and failure.

See also in this chapter: CASH OUTFLOWS EXCEEDING CASH INFLOWS, INEFFICIENT USE OF CASH, *and* INADEQUATE CASH POSITION.

PROBLEM
PAYING OUT CASH TOO SOON
SYMPTOMS

- Poor cash position.
- Impaired credit rating.
- Making full payments on accounts.

CAUSES

- Poor cash management.
- Improper cash analysis and poor decision-making.
- Lack of standardized payment procedures.
- Failure to use the most up-to-date cash planning, and computer software and cash models.

ANALYSIS

The savings in delaying cash payment should be computed. The business may earn a useful return on the cash by holding it longer.

Example: Every two weeks the company issues checks to cover payroll that average $500,000 and take three days to clear. The CFO wants to find out how much money can be saved annually if the transfer of funds from an account that pays 0.0384 percent per day (an annual rate of 14 percent) is delayed for three days.

$$\$500,000 \times (0.000384 \times 3) = \$576.$$

Savings per year = $576 x 26 payrolls per year = $14,976.

Cash models should be used in cash management to minimize the sum of the fixed costs of transactions and the opportunity cost of holding cash balances.

REPAIR

- Never pay vendors early.
- Take longer to pay tolerant creditors as long as there is no finance charge and no impairment of credit.
- Decide who should be paid first and who last.
- Deposit funds into checking and payroll accounts only when checks are expected to clear. Many full-service banks that offer customers consulting services point out structural defects in the Federal Reserve and other collection systems that allow a business to extend the payment period.
- Make partial payments or postdate checks, or both.
- Ask for more information about an invoice before paying it.
- Mail payments late in the day or on Fridays.
- Use cash models for cash management.

PREVENTION TECHNIQUES

- Centralize the payables operation so that debt may be paid at the time most beneficial to the company.
- Use payment drafts, in which payment is not made on demand. Instead, the draft is presented for collection to the bank, which in turn goes to the issuer to accept it. A draft may be used to allow for inspection before payment. When approved, the business deposits the funds. As a result, a smaller checking balance is required.
- Draw checks on remote banks.
- Mail from post offices with limited service or where mail has to go through numerous handling points. Checks can also be mailed from a location far removed from both the payee and payer banks.
- Use probability analysis to determine the expected date for checks to clear.
- Use a charge account to lengthen the time between buying goods and paying for them.
- Avoid prepaid expenses.
- Use noncash consideration, such as stock or notes, for compensation.
- Delay the frequency of payments to employees. Avoid giving cash advances for travel and entertainment or loans. Have a monthly rather than a weekly payroll. When finances are really tight, ask employees to take furloughs (e.g., two weeks off without pay) or give up a current paycheck to be paid at a later date.
- Pay commissions on sales when receivables are collected rather than when the sales are made.
- Use barter arrangements to avoid cash payments.
- Use cash flow software for day-to-day cash management, planning and analyzing cash flows, and determining payment dates.

SPILLOVER EFFECTS

The result of paying early is less cash on hand, less liquidity, a lower rate of return earned, and possibly higher financing costs. This may result in cash problems and a decline in profits.

See also in this chapter: CASH OUTFLOWS EXCEEDING CASH INFLOWS, DELAYED CUSTOMER PAYMENTS, INEFFICIENT USE OF CASH, *and* INADEQUATE CASH POSITION.

PROBLEM
CASH OUTFLOWS EXCEEDING
CASH INFLOWS

SYMPTOMS

- Declining profits.
- Cash flow problems.
- Increased use of credit lines.
- Failure to pay bills or debt on time.

CAUSES

- Slow collections from customers.
- Low profit margin.
- Paying bills before their due date.
- Failure to expedite the collection of accounts receivable.
- Failure to reduce the lag between when customers pay their bills and when the checks are converted into cash.
- Overspending.
- Excessive debt.
- Failure to fully assess a customer's credit risk.

ANALYSIS

To effectively control cash flows, management must understand the basic difference between accounting profits shown on the bottom line of the income statement and economic profits (cash flows).

REPAIR

- Speed up collections by offering discounts and relaxing credit standards—but beware of creating more bad debts.
- Stretch payables as long as possible.
- Sell off assets to reduce debt.
- Pay expenses and other obligations only at their due date.
- Buy used assets rather than new ones.

PREVENTION TECHNIQUES

- Establish a line of credit with a bank.
- Actively manage receivables.

- Spend more time on efficient management of accounts payable.
- Use cash management models that can help determine the optimal cash that a company should have available for operations. *(See above*, PAYING CASH TOO SOON, for a full discussion of cash models.)

SPILLOVER EFFECTS

When its cash outflows exceed inflows, a company may have to finance expansion at premium borrowing rates, thereby reducing profit margins. This often leads to a sacrifice of quality because the business can no longer afford extra staff, or necessary expenditures. Inadequate cash flow will also result in lower credit ratings, decline in the market price of the company's stocks and bonds, inability to make profitable investments at the right time, and, in severe cases, insolvency and bankruptcy.

See also in this chapter: DELAYED CUSTOMER PAYMENTS, GOING BROKE WHILE MAINTAINING PROFITS, INADEQUATE CASH POSITION, *and* INEFFICIENT USE OF CASH.

PROBLEM GOING BROKE WHILE MAINTAINING PROFITS

SYMPTOMS

- The company shows a profit but has no cash.
- Management mistakes accounts receivable for cash and makes daily payments for inventory, payroll, and taxes.
- The company fails to budget properly for capital expenditures and emergencies.

CAUSES

- Failure to institute an effective cash management system.
- Failure to write a realistic business plan that estimates financial needs, identifies corporate strengths and weaknesses, and sets profit goals and policies.
- Overspending and excessive debt.

ANALYSIS

The company must have a plan for cash inflows and outflows. It must also institute an effective cash collection policy.

REPAIR

- Study the cash flow cycle of the business.
- Prepare a monthly or quarterly cash budget forecast.
- Calculate current ratios to determine whether they are within the normal industry range.
- Bill credit sales promptly and maintain realistic credit policies.
- Use COD terms for chronic slow payers.

PREVENTION TECHNIQUES

- Establish both a lockbox system and regional offices for rapid processing of checks that originate at distant points.
- Obtain working capital from suppliers of merchandise, materials, and equipment by buying from suppliers who do not demand immediate payment.
- Use domestic letters of credit, whereby a bank makes a written commitment on behalf of a buyer to pay the seller for goods shipped.
- Lease an asset instead of purchasing it.
- Pay overtime to reduce the need to hire additional workers.
- Hire temporary help for peak periods to reduce compensation costs in a labor-intensive business.

SPILLOVER EFFECTS

If financing is available at all, a company with a deficient cash position will have to pay higher interest rates on loans and accept restrictions on the business. Because a company that is out of cash cannot operate effectively, its profitability will decline. Management may face a net operating loss for a given period even if cash flow has increased.

See also in this chapter: CASH OUTFLOWS EXCEEDING CASH INFLOWS, DELAYED CUSTOMER PAYMENTS, *and* INADEQUATE CASH POSITION.

PROBLEM
INEFFICIENT USE OF CASH

SYMPTOMS

- The company does not have enough cash to meet current debt obligations.
- There is more cash on hand than is necessary to cover operations, but it is not generating investment income.
- The profit margin is falling.

CAUSES

- Inefficient collection procedures.
- Poor disbursement policies.
- Buying too much inventory or too many capital assets.
- Inefficient use of tax deferral techniques.
- Overinvesting in short- or long-term assets.

ANALYSIS

A company's ability to sell what it produces and collect receivables is fundamental to its success. A cash flow statement is the best tool for measuring cash inflows and outflows. It outlines cash flows from operating, investing, and financing activities and shows the net change in cash and cash equivalents for each period.

Use comparative analysis to identify important ratios that reveal the correct collection time and the correct average inventory holding period for the business. (*See Chapter 5*: INADEQUATE LIQUIDITY *and* INADEQUATE WORKING CAPITAL.) As you study these ratios, it is important to compare them to industry norms.

Example: A company has collected the following data on average collection periods and average accounts receivable investments for two periods.

	Current	Prior
Average collection time (in days)	55	44
Average accounts receivable investment (per $1,000 in daily sales)	$55,000	$44,000

Measured against the previous collection period, in the current period there is an 11-day increase in the average collection period. This produces an $11,000 decrease in the company's cash capability for each $1,000 in daily sales. Management must also compare the company's collection time with that of competitors.

REPAIR

- Avoid expensive overinvestment in fixed assets.
- Make a reliable forecast of projected cash inflows and outflows and of their timing.
- Use a zero balance account (ZBA) to speed up cash inflows and slow down cash outflows. In a ZBA, a master account is set up to receive all checks coming into the system. As checks clear through the ZBA, funds are transferred to other accounts from the master account. Thus funds are transferred on a daily basis to cover checks that have cleared, leaving a zero balance at the end of the day.
- Have customers mail their payments to nearby collection centers to minimize mail delay.

PREVENTION TECHNIQUES

- Use billing and collection procedures that reduce the time between shipping, invoicing, and second notices.
- Take advantage of vendor discount policies for early payment.
- Use cash flow software to help prepare budgets and cash flow forecasts and to time payables.
- Anticipate the total cash capability necessary for an investment in fixed assets.

SPILLOVER EFFECTS

When cash outflows exceed cash inflows, a company may be unable to pay debts as they become due. It will then face strict loan terms from banks and stringent credit terms from vendors. Inability to pay cash dividends might affect the price of the company's stock and its ability to raise additional capital. Because a company with minimal cash availability cannot operate effectively, its profitability will decline, perhaps leading to insolvency and then bankruptcy.

See also in this chapter: CASH OUTFLOWS EXCEEDING CASH INFLOWS, DELAYED CUSTOMER PAYMENTS, INADEQUATE CASH POSITION, INADEQUATE LIQUIDITY, PAYING CASH TOO SOON, *and* SURPLUS FUNDS.

Chapter 2
Disarray in Accounts Payable and Receivable

If suppliers cannot pass increased costs on to consumers in the form of higher prices, profit margins will shrink. Moreover, while granting credit to risky customers can result in bad debt losses, on the other hand, an excessively tight credit policy will cause a loss of both new and repeat business. Financial managers must at the same time always be on guard against fraudulent transactions. There is a lot to think about in managing accounts payable and receivable.

In this chapter, we discuss the following problems:
- Vendor price increases.
- Hidden discount costs.
- Poor credit rating.
- Check-signing fraud and improper payments.
- Stringent credit requirements.

PROBLEM
VENDOR PRICE INCREASES
SYMPTOMS

- The vendor continually raises prices or raises them faster than the rate of inflation rises.
- The buyer company cannot raise its prices to absorb the increased

cost of materials and services and still make a reasonable profit.

CAUSES

- A vendor must raise prices because the costs of its raw materials, labor, and overhead have increased.
- A seller believes that its customers have to pay increased charges because it enjoys a monopoly.
- A seller feels that its product has been underpriced and decides to charge what the changing market will absorb.

ANALYSIS

- The purchasing department reports that the supplier is increasing costs with each purchase order.
- Actual costs exceed budgeted costs for the period under review.
- Total expenditures for a given product are substantially higher than they were for the same period in the preceding year.
- Management has determined that it cannot continue to raise the price of its product or service without losing sales and market share to competitors.

REPAIR

- Form a joint venture to manufacture the product or provide the service with another company that has the same production requirements.
- Try to enter into a barter arrangement, trading your company's product or service for the seller's merchandise or service.
- If possible, buy the supplier.
- Find an alternative supplier.
- Offer to help another company build its capacity to supply the goods or services that your company needs.
- Make the goods or produce the services yourself.
- Substitute another product or service for the current product or service you currently sell.

PREVENTION TECHNIQUES

- Accumulate stocks of supplies and raw materials.
- Enter into futures contracts for delivery at a later date at a set price.
- Enter into long-term supply arrangements.

- Review trade publications for potential problems and alternate suppliers.
- Use vertical integration to reduce the price and the supply risk of raw materials.
- Have your engineers and production managers redesign the product to reduce manufacturing costs so that the product can still be sold at the same price. If this cannot be done, redesign the product so that another part or a different service can be supplied by another company.
- Increase the selling price of current products to test whether a new price has a negative impact on sales. (If the product is manufactured, consumers may associate a higher price with a better-quality product and may be willing to pay more.)

SPILLOVER EFFECTS

If an increased selling price causes sales to fall, the profitability of the business may remain flat or even decline. The higher selling price may also diminish customer loyalty to the company's other products, resulting in a drop in sales and earnings. This may adversely affect market share and the company's ability to maintain future operations. If costs of supplies and raw materials increase, profitability will decrease in any case, however, unless selling prices are also increased. Cash flow will diminish because of the higher costs.

If the cost of raw materials increases rapidly, production cutbacks may be necessary, resulting in a lower sales volume for the company's products or services. If customers become dissatisfied, the company may lose them to competitors. A company without alternative raw material or service sources possesses higher risk and uncertainty with respect to its future earnings.

PROBLEM
HIDDEN DISCOUNT COSTS
SYMPTOM

Failure to take a cash discount offered by suppliers who sell on short-term credit.

CAUSE

A lack of financial sophistication or a lack of ready cash.

ANALYSIS

An account payable is a spontaneous source of funds. Trade credit is usually extended for 30 to 60 days. Many firms try to extend the time for payment to take advantage of this additional short-term financing. On the other hand, creditors encourage early payment by offering a cash discount. If management has not taken advantage of a discount opportunity by paying within the discount period, it has lost an opportunity cost or the return available from an alternative use of the funds. Compare the cost of payment within the discount period with the cost of borrowing money.

The standard formula for computing the opportunity cost is as follows:

$$\text{Opportunity cost} = \frac{\text{Discount forgone}}{\text{Use of proceeds}} \quad x \quad \frac{360}{\text{Days use of money}}$$

Example: X Corporation buys $500,000 of merchandise on credit terms of 2/10, net/30. The company does not pay within 10 days and thus loses the $10,000 ($500,000 x 2 percent) discount.

$$\text{Opportunity cost} = \frac{0.02 \times \$500,000}{0.98 \times \$500,000} \quad x \frac{360}{20} = \frac{\$10,000 \times 180}{\$490,000} = 36.7\%.$$

The cost of using the $490,000 for 20 more days is 36.7 percent. Because this is an excessive rate, management would be better off borrowing the $490,000 at the prime interest rate and getting the discount.

REPAIR

Compute the opportunity cost of not taking the discount. If it is excessively high, pay within the prescribed cash discount period.

PREVENTION TECHNIQUES

- Have adequate cash on hand or the ability to borrow on short notice to get the funds to pay suppliers within the discount period.
- Coordinate purchases and discount terms after determining the cash cycles of the business and the availability of money.

SPILLOVER EFFECTS

Failure to take a discount is an opportunity cost, resulting eventually in a larger cash payment and thus reducing cash on hand and increasing the cost of financing operations. The net effect is to lower liquidity and profitability.

PROBLEM
POOR CREDIT RATING

SYMPTOM

A firm's credit rating has been lowered. No credit is available to it.

CAUSES

- Market conditions.
- Excessive business risk.
- Poor management.
- The product mix.
- Continuous operating losses.
- Foreseeable future economic problems in the company's line of business.
- Excessive obsolete assets.
- Foreign competition.
- Government action.
- Failure to make a required payment on long-term debt.
- Excessive interest and labor costs.
- Overexpansion or diversification into areas in which the company has no experience.
- Cash flow problems.
- Generally deficient financial position.

ANALYSIS

- Evaluate the financial statement and the performance of the enterprise as a whole.
- Conduct horizontal, vertical, and ratio analyses.
- Calculate trend percentages (a form of horizontal analysis).
- Determine whether sales, income, and expenses are increasing or decreasing over time, and ascertain why.

- Study the reports on the industry and the economy in business publications.
- Learn what brokerage research reports have to say about the company.
- Compare the company's operating figures with industry norms and the figures for competitors.
- Study the company's cash flow statement.
- Calculate the liquidity and profitability ratios, which reflect a company's ability to pay current liabilities, sell inventory and collect receivables, pay long-term debt, and remain profitable.
- Examine earnings per share.

REPAIR

- Bring in outside consultants to recommend ways the performance of management could be improved.
- Review the financial statements for low-quality assets and excessive operating costs.
- Evaluate production facilities for possible replacement or disposal. Study foreign competition, so that you can either compete better or form an operating partnership with foreign competitors to gain their expertise.
- Drop unprofitable items.
- Sell or spin off subsidiaries that have not shown a profit over time.
- Try to restructure the company's debt and capital structure.
- Renegotiate union contracts for give-backs.
- Approach creditors to modify the company's obligations to repay long-term debt.
- Reorganize to reduce diversification and enable management to gain better operating and cost control.
- If government actions are pending against the company, try to seek an out-of-court settlement to avoid negative publicity.
- Reexamine the employee benefits package to attract and keep experienced personnel.
- Consider acquiring another company that has established markets and management capability that would enable you to expand into new geographic or areas.

PREVENTION TECHNIQUES

- Hammer out a new corporate strategy. This requires a long-range study of the market threats and opportunities facing the company, an assessment of the company's own strengths and weaknesses, and setting profit goals to be achieved by each unit of the company.
- Adopt cost-cutting procedures. Create a cash budget that outlines the financial constraints the company faces and develop reasonable alternative proposals.
- Allocate resources so that management has what it needs to achieve its profit goals.
- Revise capital and operating budgets. The capital budget will be used to purchase new and more efficient long-lived equipment. The operating budget will reflect expenditures for recurring costs, such as materials and salaries.

SPILLOVER EFFECTS

The market price of the company's stock will decline. Credit will be more difficult to obtain and more expensive if it is obtained. A firm with whose credit rating and price per share have both dropped can become a takeover candidate.

PROBLEM
CHECK FRAUD AND
IMPROPER PAYMENTS

SYMPTOMS

- Individuals within the company are forging checks.
- Cash disbursements are made to nonexistent suppliers or payees.
- Liabilities are unpaid, overpaid, or paid twice.
- The company receives an excessive number of late payment notices, resulting in both interest charges from suppliers and penalties from governmental agencies.
- An audit reveals expenditures well above what is considered normal or has been budgeted.
- Independent auditors discover fraud and embezzlement.
- The company issues unnumbered checks that are not recorded in the accounting records.

- Disbursements are under the control of one individual.
- The cash balance on the book is more than the cash on hand and in the company's cash account.
- A bank reconciliation by the independent accountants reveals discrepancies between the book and the bank balances.
- Endorsements are missing from the backs of checks.
- Checks are written with spaces so that they can be later altered by payees and subsequent holders.
- An abnormal number of checks are payable to cash.
- Many interbank transfers cover cash shortages in the statements received from the bank.
- Bills are not checked to see whether they accurately describe items purchased, pricing, or total amounts received.

CAUSES

- Inadequate internal control procedures.
- Employee fraud.

ANALYSIS

Although the cash balance is not normally a major figure on the balance sheet. the dollar amounts that flow through the account are usually greater than those flowing through any other account. Moreover, cash, as the most liquid of all assets, is easily vulnerable to theft. Management must assess the risk that errors and irregularities may materially affect the company's financial statements.

REPAIR

- Review and test all internal control procedures.
- Separate functions. Assign to different people responsibility for authorizing payment, signing the checks, and recording them in the accounting records.
- Make sure someone else is responsible for checking bills and payroll records.
- Have the independent auditors perform a monthly bank reconciliation and compare signatures on the checks with the list of authorized check-signers. Examine endorsements to see that the check is endorsed by the payee and that there are no unusual second endorsements.

- Compare all canceled checks for several accounting periods with the accounting records to verify date, number, payee, and amount.
- Investigate if there is a large number of checks payable to cash and checks long outstanding.
- Seek reimbursement from the company's insurer for any losses sustained.
- Prosecute all perpetrators and announce this policy to the entire company.

PREVENTION TECHNIQUES

- Review, evaluate, and if necessary install new internal control procedures for cash disbursement.
- Reconcile bank statements every month.
- Account for all check numbers issued during the month ending on the audit date.
- Review all interbank transfers.
- Perform a proof of cash.
- Trace all disbursements to actual purchases and to the employee payroll.
- Review all purchase requisitions to see that the company actually needed supplies and services bought, there was authorization for the purchase, and the goods or services were actually received.
- Keep the check-writing machine under lock and key when not in use.
- Require more than one signature for checks for large amounts.
- Bond all employees who sign checks and record disbursements.
- Learn whether employees own or operate enterprises that have dealings with the company, thus creating the opportunity for illegal collusion.

SPILLOVER EFFECTS

The lack of effective check authorization and disbursement procedures will mean that nonexistent assets and expenses are recorded. Working capital will be inadequate due to theft of cash. Financial position and operating results may be misstated. This will lead to incorrect financial management decisions, audits, and review by governmental agencies.

Stockholder derivative suits will be directed against the board of directors and corporate executives for mismanagement. Investors may sue the company for losses sustained because of the theft of cash and the preparation of erroneous financial statements. Bankruptcy is possible if thefts continue uncontrolled.

See Chapter22: RECORDKEEPING ERRORS.

PROBLEM
TOO STRINGENT
CREDIT REQUIREMENTS

Financial management is often faced with a decision of whether to give credit to marginal customers. How it makes that decision is very important.

SYMPTOMS

- Lost sales.
- Loss of customers in higher-risk categories.
- Declining profitability.

CAUSES

- Management conservatism.
- Poor financial management and analysis.
- Deficient credit analysis and evaluation.
- Problems in the economy.
- Industry difficulties.

ANALYSIS

A too-tight credit policy is indicated by:
- Declining sales.
- Fewer uncollectible accounts.
- High accounts receivable turnover (annual credit sales divided by average accounts receivable).
- Short collection period (360 days divided by the accounts receivable turnover rate).

REPAIR

Relax the policy and give credit when the profitability of the potential additional sales exceeds the additional costs associated with these sales, such as higher bad debts, the opportunity cost of tying up funds in receivables for longer time, and increased clerical costs for servicing an additional customer base.

Determine the policy based on rating systems like Dun & Bradstreet's, but do not use the same standard for all customers. Organize your credit policies by category.

PREVENTION TECHNIQUES

- Direct credit management to think more deeply about the benefits of liberalizing credit. Increased profitability, stronger future business, and improved public relations.
- Have credit approved only by experienced and realistic credit managers.

SPILLOVER EFFECTS

- Loss of market share and competitive advantage.
- Lack of growth.
- Lower net income.
- Worsened balance sheet position.

Chapter 3
Inventory Shortfalls

Failure to turn over merchandise quickly will result in higher carrying costs and obsolescence of the goods. Tying up money in inventory balances sacrifices a return on that money.

On the other hand, inadequate stocking will result in lost sales and may cause customers to switch to other suppliers. Failure to control inventory ordering and storage costs will adversely affect profitability. Inadequate internal controls can invite theft of inventory. Inaccurate records and miscounts will fail to reveal how much inventory actually exists. If production or supplier schedules are not adhered to, facilities may be idle and cause inventory balances to vary, with the result that the firm is often out of certain items and loses sales.

These are not the only inventory problems. Poor-quality goods will be reflected in product returns and discounts as well as in loss of customer satisfaction and loyalty. A lack of inventory storage space will make it harder to keep the right balances on hand.

The following problems are addressed in this chapter:
- Low turnover of merchandise.
- Deficient inventory balances.
- Excessive inventory ordering and carrying costs.
- Ordering incorrect quantities of inventory.
- High rate of stockout.

- Theft of inventory.
- Miscounted inventory.
- Inaccurate inventory records.
- High rate of product obsolescence.
- Manufacturing schedules missed.
- Poor-quality goods produced.
- Lack of inventory storage space.
- Delayed receipt of new inventory.

PROBLEM
LOW TURNOVER OF MERCHANDISE
SYMPTOMS

- Slow sales.
- Unusual buildup of inventory either at the plant or at the whole-sale or retail level (buildup occurs when inventory increases faster than sales).
- Lack of demand for products.
- Deficiencies in the product line.
- Technological obsolescence.

CAUSES

The usual reason for low turnover is lack of demand, which may be due to:

- High prices.
- Poor marketing.
- Increased competition.
- Inventory purchases that exceed production and sales requirements.
- Ineffective advertising.
- Negative publicity.

It is also possible that inventory previously written off but still on hand, may have been included in the count of ending inventory.

ANALYSIS

- Determine the inventory turnover by category as well as by department. The turnover ratio is calculated as follows:

• A seasonal business should check the inventory turnover rate monthly or quarterly.

Example: The Fremont Corporation has the following data for the year:

$$\frac{\text{Cost of goods sold}}{\text{Average inventory}}$$

Cost of goods sold	= $4,500,000
Beginning inventory January 1	= $1,000,000
Ending inventory December 31	= $ 800,000

The inventory turnover would be five, calculated as follows:

Average inventory:

Beginning inventory	= $1,000,000
Ending inventory	= $ 800,000
Beginning plus ending inventory	= $1,800,000

$$\text{Average inventory for year} = \frac{\$1,800,000}{2} = \$900,000.$$

$$\frac{\text{Cost of goods sold}}{\text{Average inventory}} = \frac{\$4,500,000}{\$900,000} = 5.$$

Inventory turnover measures the number of times a company sells its average inventory during the year. A high turnover indicates a product that is selling well. A low turnover indicates lack of demand. Yet a high turnover may not necessarily be the best situation. It may instead indicate that the company is not keeping enough inventory on hand to meet sales and production demands. Having insufficient inventory on hand can mean lost production time and lost sales. Also, the turnover rate may be unusually high when the firm makes the calculation using its natural year-end, since at that time the inventory balance will be exceptionally low.

In some cases, a low turnover rate may be appropriate, as when higher inventory is built up in anticipation of rapidly rising prices, or when a new product line has been introduced for which the advertising effects have not yet been felt.

The inventory turnover ratio varies from industry to industry. It indicates how quickly a company is selling its inventory and whether the inventory is readily marketable. By comparing the turnover ratio with other companies in the same industry, financial management can determine whether inventory on hand is reasonable and is sufficient to meet sales and production demands. A sharp decline in the ratio over a long period mandates corrective action by management.

- The number of days inventory is held should also be computed and the age of inventory compared to the industry norm as well as to the firm's experience.
- Then, determine the percentage of inventory that is comprised of slow moving, obsolete, and out-of-favor merchandise.
- A decline in raw materials, coupled with an increase in work-in-process and finished goods, may indicate a future production slowdown.

REPAIR

- Compare the company's inventory turnover with other companies in the same industry and with industry averages.
- Question the sales force about why sales appear to be declining.
- Determine whether the company's advertising is effective.
- Identify and discard damaged or obsolete inventory.
- Cancel commitments to purchase additional quantities of similar items.
- Check for errors in the inventory records.
- Count all items on hand before calculating turnover.
- Ascertain the ideal inventory turnover number and adjust inventory on hand to meet this number.
- Determine whether previously written-off inventory may still be being counted in ending inventory.
- Correct the records as required.

PREVENTION TECHNIQUES

- Establish a standard of management performance by product line and compare the standards to other companies in the same industry.
- Break down all items into different categories and calculate the turnover for each category. If the ratio is an average of many

types of goods, it may be difficult to determine which goods are selling and which are not.

- Monitor company turnover against competitors and the industry average and adjust inventory as needed.

SPILLOVER EFFECTS

Low inventory turnover increases the possibility of inventory obsolescence, lost sales, and theft. Excess inventory increases the costs of insurance, storage, and payroll, reducing net earnings. Excess inventory also ties up funds that could be invested for a return.

PROBLEM
DEFICIENT INVENTORY BALANCES
SYMPTOMS

- Production cutbacks.
- Inability to satisfy customers.

CAUSE

This problem tends to result from failure to use an inventory model or a computerized inventory system, so that raw materials are ordered at the wrong time and in the wrong amounts.

ANALYSIS

The reorder point (ROP) tells you the inventory point at which a new order should be placed. However, to use ROP you must know the lead-time it takes to receive an order after placing it.

Reorder point = Lead time x Average usage per unit of time.

If you need a safety stock, add this amount to the ROP model.

Example: The company uses 6,400 units evenly throughout the year, and there is a constant lead time for order delivery of one week. There are 50 working weeks in the year. The ROP is computed as follows:

$$\text{Reorder point} = 1 \text{ week x } \frac{6,400}{50 \text{ weeks}} = 1 \text{ x } 128 = 128 \text{ units.}$$

When the inventory level drops to 128 units, a new order should be placed.

Figure 3.1 shows how this system works when the order quantity equals 400 units.

FIGURE 3.1. Basic Inventory System

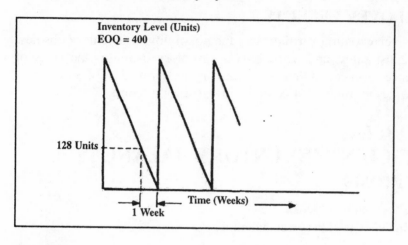

REPAIR

Use an inventory model to determine when to reorder.

PREVENTION TECHNIQUES

Analyze previous shortages, how long it usually takes to get for delivery, seasonal customer demands, what the usage has been, and the condition of the manufacturing facilities.

SPILLOVER EFFECTS

- Losing current and prospective customers.
- Manufacturing delays.
- Inactivity in productive resources.
- Lower earnings.

See also in this chapter: DELAYED RECEIPT OF NEW INVENTORY, EXCESSIVE ORDERING AND CARRYING COSTS, HIGH RATE OF INVENTORY STOCKOUT, *and* ORDERING INCORRECT QUANTITIES.

PROBLEM
EXCESSIVE ORDERING AND CARRYING COSTS

SYMPTOMS

- Carrying costs—for warehousing, handling, property tax, and insurance—are high because of an inventory buildup.
- High costs per order—for preparing the purchase order, receiving goods, freight, and processing payments—prompt a higher order quantity each time.
- Overstocking results in inventory obsolescence and theft.

CAUSES

- Improper inventory management, planning, and control.
- Excessive inventory balances and lack of cost control.
- An inefficient purchasing department.

ANALYSIS

There is a trade-off between order size and carrying cost. The higher the quantity ordered, the higher the carrying cost—but the lower the ordering cost.

$$\text{Total number of orders} = \frac{S}{EOQ}$$

where S = Total usage.

EOQ = Economic order quantity. The optimum amount to order each time to minimize total costs (ordering and carrying).

$$\text{Total order cost} = \frac{EOQ}{2} \times O.$$

where O = Cost per order.

$$\text{Total carrying cost} = \frac{EOQ}{2} \times C.$$

where C = Carrying cost per unit.

$$\frac{EOQ}{2} = \text{Average inventory quantity for the period.}$$

$$\text{Total inventory cost} = \frac{(S \times O)}{EOQ} + \frac{(EOQ \times C)}{2}$$

Compare trends in carrying costs and ordering costs over time. Calculate the ratios of carrying cost to inventory, carrying cost to sales, ordering cost to inventory, and ordering cost to sales. Higher ratios may signal problems.

Inventory levels are also influenced by short-term interest rates. As interest rates increase, it costs more to finance and hold inventory.

REPAIR

- Hold less physical inventory.
- Place fewer orders.
- Use inventory models to determine the optimal inventory level necessary to minimize related costs.
- Reduce production until inventory levels are adjusted properly.
- Use the just-in-time (JIT) system of managing inventory, in which to reduce inventory costs the company buys and produces in very small quantities just in time for use.
- Buy large volumes of high usage items to get greater discounts.
- Streamline clerical operations.
- Rent cheaper storage space.
- Move to a locality with lower property taxes.
- Reduce insurance costs by altering the deductible, changing policy limits, or switching to a new carrier.
- Place stringent internal controls on inventory to guard against theft.

PREVENTION TECHNIQUES

- Establish policies to keep the inventory balance optimized to reduce costs.
- Use the ROP model to time your orders.
- Compute average sales volume per square foot of shelf space, and replace products whose sales are grossly below the average.
- Redesign packaging to save costs.

SPILLOVER EFFECTS

High costs associated with inventory will lower profit margins. Deficient inventory planning will cause inventory losses due to causes like oversupply, obsolescence, and perishability.

See also in this chapter: DEFICIENT INVENTORY BALANCES, HIGH RATE OF INVENTORY STOCKOUT, *and* ORDERING INCORRECT QUANTITIES.

PROBLEM
ORDERING INCORRECT QUANTITIES
SYMPTOMS

- Overstocking.
- Obsolescence.
- Shortages.
- Back orders.
- Production slowdowns.
- Theft of inventory.

CAUSES

- The wrong amount is ordered because of poor inventory management.
- The company is not using inventory models.

ANALYSIS

One technique that can be used to order the right amount is the EOQ model, which determines the order size that minimizes the sum of carrying and ordering costs. The EOQ model is most suitable for a pure inventory system. That is, for single-item, single-stage inventory decisions for which joint costs and constraints can be ignored. The model does not consider quantity discounts, which may be unrealistic—typically, the more you order, the lower the unit price.

EOQ assumes that demand is known with certainty and will remain constant throughout the year. Order cost and unit carrying costs are also assumed to be constant. Since demand and lead time (the interval between placing an order and its delivery) are assumed to be determinable, there are no shortage costs.

EOQ is computed as follows:

$$EOQ = \sqrt{\frac{2 \text{ (Annual demand) (Ordering cost)}}{\text{Carrying cost per unit}}}$$

$$\text{Total inventory cost} = \text{Carrying cost per unit x } \frac{EOQ}{2} + \text{Order cost x } \frac{\text{Annual}}{EOQ}$$

$$\text{Total number of orders per year} = \frac{\text{Annual demand}}{EOQ}$$

Example: Oakman, Inc. buys steel at $40 per set. Oakman will need 6,400 sets evenly throughout the year. The goal of management is a 16 percent return on its inventory investment (cost of capital). In addition, rent, insurance, taxes, etc. for each set in inventory comes to $ 1.60. The order cost is $100.

Carrying cost per set = $1.60 + .16 ($40) = $8.00. Thus,

$$EOQ = \sqrt{\frac{2(6,400)(100)}{\$8.00}} = \sqrt{16,000} = 400 \text{ sets.}$$

$$
\begin{aligned}
\text{Total inventory costs} \ &= \$8.00 \ (400/2) + \$100 \ (6,400/400) \\
&= \$1,600 + \$1,600 = \$3,200.
\end{aligned}
$$

$$
\begin{aligned}
\text{Total number of annual orders} \ &= 6,400/400 \\
&= 16 \text{ orders.}
\end{aligned}
$$

REPAIR

Use the EOQ model to determine order size and frequency of orders. Increase order size to take advantage of quantity discounts or lower prices.

PREVENTION TECHNIQUES

- Improve forecasting and recordkeeping.
- Use EOQ formulas.
- Hire an experienced inventory manager.

SPILLOVER EFFECTS

Incorrect order size leads either to an inventory buildup or to inadequate inventory. An inventory buildup results in excess carrying costs, a drain on cash flow, obsolescence and spoilage, increased likelihood of theft, and therefore lower profitability. An inadequate inventory balance will result in lost sales and customer dissatisfaction.

See also in this chapter: DEFICIENT INVENTORY BALANCES, EXCESSIVE ORDERING AND CARRYING COSTS, *and* HIGH RATE OF INVENTORY STOCKOUT.

PROBLEM
HIGH RATE OF INVENTORY STOCKOUT

SYMPTOM

There is no merchandise on hand to fill customer orders.

CAUSE

Poor inventory planning and control is often due to inaccurate estimates of sales or materials requirements.

ANALYSIS

When lead time and demand are uncertain, you must carry extra units of inventory, called safety stock, to protect against possible stockouts. Safety stock is the minimum inventory amount needed to serve as a buffer against unusual product demand or unanticipated delivery problems.

Safety stock is optimal when the increased carrying cost equals the opportunity cost that would be caused by a stockout. (The increased carrying cost equals the carrying cost per unit times units of safety stock.)

Stockout cost = Number of orders (S/EOQ) x Stockout units x Unit stockout cost x Probability of a stockout.

Example: You use 250,000 units a year. Each order is for 25,000 units. Stockout is 4,000 units. The tolerable stockout probability is 25 percent. The per-unit stockout cost is $4. The carrying cost per unit is $8.

Stockout cost = $\dfrac{250,000}{25,000}$ x 250,000 x 4,000 x \$4.00 x 0.25 = \$40,000.

Amount of safety stock needed = $\dfrac{\text{Stockout cost}}{\text{Carrying cost per unit}}$

$$= \frac{\$40,000}{\$8} = 5,000 \text{ units.}$$

Where   L = Lead time.

F = Stockout acceptance factor.

$$EOP = SL + F \sqrt{S(EOQ)(L)}.$$

A stockout cost is estimated at \$12 per set. The carrying cost is \$8 per set. The reorder point is 128 sets without safety stock. Computation of safety stock is shown in Table 3.1, which shows that total costs are minimized at \$1,200 when a safety stock of 150 sets is maintained. Thus, ROP = 128 sets + 150 sets, or 278 sets.

TABLE 3.1. COMPUTING OPTIMAL AMOUNT OF SAFETY STOCK

Safety Stock in Units	Stockout and Probability	Average Stockout in Units	Average Stockout Costs	Number of Orders	Total Annual Stockout Costs	Carrying Costs	Total
0	50 with 0.2 100 with 0.1 150 with 0.1	35*	\$420+	16	\$6,720+	0	\$6,720
50	50 with 0.1 100 with 0.1	15	180	16	2,880	400	3,290
100	50 with 0.1	5	60	16	960	800	1,760
150	0	0	0	16	0	1,200	1,200

*50(0.2) + 100(0.1) + 150(0.1) = 10 + 10 + 15 = 35 units.
+35 units x \$12.00 = \$420.
\$420 x 16 times = \$6,720.
§50 units x \$8.00 = \$400.

REPAIR

- Order additional inventory of selected items to guard against stockouts.
- Introduce computerized systems, such as material requirements planning (MRP), to have enough materials on hand to meet expected future demand.

PREVENTION TECHNIQUES

Use the formulas given above to determine stockout cost, safety stock, and ROP.

SPILLOVER EFFECTS

- Lost sales.
- Reduced profits.
- Disgruntled customers.
- Idle machines.
- Disrupted production scheduling.

See also in this chapter DEFICIENT INVENTORY BALANCES *and* EXCESSIVE ORDERING AND CARRYING COSTS.

PROBLEM
THEFT

SYMPTOM

Inventory on hand is less than what the accounting records indicate it should be.

Causes

- Lack of physical safeguards.
- Improper internal controls.
- Inaccurate accounting records.
- Failure to record inventory purchases.
- Ineffective method of counting inventory.

ANALYSIS

Management and outside auditors have performed a physical count of the inventory, determining what is actually owned by the company and what is held in a custodial capacity for other companies. The amount on the books does not reconcile with the amount actually on hand. Shortages may require immediate purchase of the missing items to meet urgent customer demands, thereby exposing the buyer to higher prices plus premium transportation costs for rush delivery of the goods. Thefts thus create additional unnecessary expense.

REPAIR

- Review internal control procedures.
- Conduct training programs for each inventory procedure.
- Have each inventory item assigned to a different area with a specific person in charge.
- Lock up all merchandise.
- Install a lock system that permit limited access to low-cost inventory by one authorized individual and a two-key system requiring two or more authorized employees to access higher-value inventory.
- File insurance claims to recover the cost of stolen inventory.
- Carefully mark Do Not Inventory and if possible segregate all material that was sold before the end of the accounting period to avoid including it in the ending count.

PREVENTION TECHNIQUES

- Install proper internal control procedures.
- Inspect all items received by the company to check whether the amount matches the vendor's bill.
- Establish a system whereby different employees accept goods. Transfer the goods to the warehouse, other storage area, or production line. Keep inventory records and ship merchandise to customers.
- Make unannounced spot counts of inventory on hand.
- Make the employee in charge explain any discrepancies.
- Periodically change locks or security codes in storage areas.
- Make everyone responsible for theft-awareness, so that any employee can furnish information without fear of reprisal.
- Encourage employees to report possible weaknesses in the inventory security system.
- Bond all employees associated with physical storage and recordkeeping of inventory.
- Maintain a well-prepared perpetual computerized inventory sys-

tem to better control inventory.

- Make sure all purchases are validly authorized.
- Physically recount a percentage of all major balances of inventory and a small percentage of the lower value items.
- Question management and employees about goods held by others on consignment or in a warehouse at another location.
- Use the commonsense test if the count looks suspicious.
- Make out a zero-quantity tag for items with an assigned location but no parts.
- Consolidate all similar items to expedite accurate control and count.
- Write up an inventory policy specifying the purpose of the inventory program, responsibilities in the chain of command, why an accurate inventory count is important, and examples of errors, their causes, and their negative impact on the company's financial status.
- Create a job description for the inventory coordinator, who should have experience in creating inventory policy and writing inventory procedures, including the counting of ending inventory.
- Review the ending inventory balances, check the accuracy of the number of parts received, appraise employee performance in the periodic counting of inventory, and monitor inventory balances for discrepancies.
- Use a uniform inventory ticket for listing the actual amount on hand. Use one tag for each inventory item. Number all tags and account for missing ones at the end of the count. Have employees initial the ticket.
- If corrections make tags illegible, mark them "void," write a new tag, and give voided and unused tags to the inventory coordinator. Number all inventory sheets and account for all missing sheets at the end of the count. Double-count all high-value items.
- Be sure employees understand instructions for taking inventory. Review the results of the final count for deviations from what is considered a normal ending balance for specific parts or groups of parts.

- Supervise inventory carefully. Insist that there will be no requisitions without the permission of the inventory coordinator. Make sure that inventory that must be moved during the counting period is not counted twice. No material should be moved within an area without authorization by the area supervisor.
- Post instructions for calibration and weigh-counting directly on the scales.

SPILLOVER EFFECTS

Theft of inventory can cause serious erosion of profits to the point of insolvency. The company will also lose customers if management has told them certain inventory is on hand when in fact it is missing. Management could be sued by stockholders for incompetence and negligence regarding inventory, a major asset on the balance sheet. The disclosure of employee fraud will also increase audit fees and insurance premiums.

PROBLEM
MISCOUNTED INVENTORY

SYMPTOMS

- Unusually large balances in obsolete goods.
- Small balances in current inventory parts.
- No balances for parts that are usually in stock at all times.
- Inventory held in a custodial capacity for other owners and counted as part of the ending inventory.

CAUSES

- Inexperienced help.
- Lack of training in counting inventory.
- Improper procedures for inventory.
- Shortage of qualified personnel.
- Improper entries.
- Math errors.

ANALYSIS

- Assign an experienced and reliable person to review all inventory tickets and forms for accuracy in describing and counting items.

- Have another experienced employee double-check all inventory tickets for correct quantities.
- Correct any tickets found to contain errors.

REPAIR

- Establish a formal procedure for classifying and counting inventory.
- Employ only experienced people familiar with the raw materials used in production to count the inventory.

SPILLOVER EFFECTS

If ending inventory is incorrect, the company's understanding of its profits, balance sheet, tax liabilities, current ratio, and working capital will also be incorrect.

PROBLEM
INACCURATE INVENTORY
RECORDS SYMPTOMS

- Inability to meet delivery promises.
- Uneven production due to lack of inventory.
- Excessive machine downtime because of material shortages.
- Incomplete records.
- Duplication of effort.
- Unproductive recordkeeping time.
- Theft of inventory.
- Increase in audit fees.
- Confusion caused by inventory held for another company that is erroneously included in the company's own ending inventory.·
- Overlapping accounting functions.

CAUSES

- Incompetent or inexperienced accounting staff.
- Shortage of qualified employees.
- Lack of internal controls and audits.
- Deficient organizational structure.
- Failure to keep records current.
- Failure to identify inventory consigned to the company by other companies for resale.

ANALYSIS

Inaccurate inventory records affect management decisions and net income. Management must analyze the inventory in terms of items on hand, service level—the percentage of time items will be on the shelf to fill a customer's order—and the incidence and dollar amount of inventory theft. Recordkeeping errors misstate inventory.

REPAIR

- Institute internal controls to safeguard assets and assure the integrity of the accounting system.
- Check for inconsistencies in inventory procedures.
- Improve unsatisfactory procedures.
- Undertake internal and external audits to confirm accuracy of the records. Any accounting errors discovered should be corrected immediately.
- Ask an independent CPA firm to evaluate the accounting system and make written recommendations for improvement.
- Install computerized inventory software packages and a bar code system to improve accuracy and timeliness of the records.

PREVENTION TECHNIQUES

- Train the accounting staff' thoroughly in how to operate the computer program and the bar-code system.
- Make sure employees are both honest and competent.
- Institute a clear separation of duties to ensure proper internal control.
- Make sure all accounting procedures are properly authorized.
- Make sure that all transactions are properly documented and reviewed, with specific authorizations for certain types of transactions.
- Secure both physical assets and records.
- Create safeguards to prevent misappropriation of inventory.
- Have both internal and external auditors check independently to ensure that inventory balances on hand agree with accounting records.
- Assign designated items of inventory to specific areas for easy identification. The person responsible for a particular inventory storage area will be called upon to explain any discrepancies.

SPILLOVER EFFECTS

If the inventory accounting system is inadequate or inefficient, it will not generate reliable information and financial decisions based on the inaccurate data will be faulty. Cost of goods sold and ending inventory, both major components of both the balance sheet and income statement, will be wrong. As a result, the financial position and operating results of the company may be misstated. This will lead to more poor decisions, audits and review by various governmental agencies, and lawsuits by stockholders, investors, and creditors—the kind of things that negatively affect the market price of outstanding shares and subsequent public offerings.

See in Chapter 12: RECORDKEEPING ERRORS.

PROBLEM
HIGH RATE OF
PRODUCT OBSOLESCENCE

SYMPTOMS

- Low inventory turnover.
- Slow sales despite large markdowns.
- Competing models with advanced features.

CAUSES

- Perishable, specialized, faddish, or high-tech products.
- Buying too much without specific production goals.
- Errors in production requirements.
- Sudden lack of demand for the product.
- Purchase of a large amount of goods because the terms are advantageous.

ANALYSIS

Evaluate the age of items in inventory and write down older and less desirable merchandise.

REPAIR

- Create an advisory group familiar with the manufacturing requirements of the business to advise top management on policymaking

decisions.
- Determine what is a proper level of inventory based on the company's turnover and production objectives.
- Set a specific inventory level for production and sales purposes.
- Determine what in inventory is damaged, slow-moving, overstocked, out-of-style, or obsolete and also see if the company is committed to buy additional quantities of similar items. If it can be done, cancel the commitments.
- Sell off obsolete inventory at the market price. If the inventory has no value, donate it to a charity to generate goodwill and favorable publicity. Its disposal will reduce the costs of storage, warehousing, insurance coverage, and payroll incurred in keeping records and safeguarding it.
- Determine whether recent deliveries of inventory no longer needed can be returned to vendors for partial or complete credit.

PREVENTION TECHNIQUES

- Set an appropriate inventory level. An excellent method to use is the targeted inventory method, under which total inventory issues in dollars for the prior year are divided by the inventory turnover desired by management. The result is the inventory target amount, which is then compared to the actual inventory on hand. If the actual amount exceeds the targeted amount, the difference is deemed excess inventory, subject to possible obsolescence.

  Example:
  Total inventory purchases last year = $5,000,000.
  Turnover desired by management = 25.
  Actual inventory at year-end = $222,000.

  The excess inventory on hand at year-end subject to possible obsolescence would be $22,000, calculated as follows

  Inventory target ($5,000,000 ÷ 25) = $200,000
  Actual inventory at year-end = $222,000
  Excess inventory subject to possible obsolescence = $ 22,000

- Appoint an inventory reduction team to review all areas and activities affecting inventory levels anywhere in the company. Have the team analyze inventory management problems and suggest immediate steps to reduce inventories.

- Classify inventory target levels as desirable, permissible, and undesirable.
- Carefully reduce inventory to a predetermined minimum to avoid affecting production or customer service.
- Ask management to determine the inventory level that is optimal for maintaining the production schedule and serving customers.
- Study industry trends in product changes, supplies of raw materials, and manufacturing processes.
- Negotiate with suppliers the most liberal possible return policy on purchases.

SPILLOVER EFFECTS

Writing down obsolete inventory will increase the cost of goods sold and will lower earnings.

PROBLEM
MISSED MANUFACTURING SCHEDULES
SYMPTOMS

- Production quotas and schedules are not met.
- Sales orders are not filled because completed product is not available for immediate shipment.
- Sales are declining.
- The company begins to get a reputation for unreliability.
- Delay in receiving raw materials results in significant downtime for both workers and machines.
- Production facilities are obsolete.
- Workers are unproductive.

CAUSES

- Inexperienced personnel.
- Insufficient in product technological innovations.
- Introduction of new production machinery and methods.
- Failure to forecast inventory requirements and keep purchases at a correct level.
- Stockouts of required parts.
- Excessive employee absences and turnover.

- High rate of customer turnover and order cancellations.
- Theft of vital materials.

ANALYSIS

Efficient companies review their production proficiency every three months to keep up with technological changes in the marketplace, new production equipment, and changes in availability of raw materials and of experienced personnel. An effective review will appraise organizational structure, production objectives, inventory control methods, effectiveness of production departments, and accuracy of the accounting records.

REPAIR

- Determine weaknesses in each sector of the company that affects production.
- Evaluate the performance of production managers, supervisors, and workers.
- Establish safety stock levels.
- Make sure that rejected material purchases are quickly returned to vendors or reprocessed.
- Monitor employee absenteeism and turnover.
- Evaluate the performance of all personnel associated with inventory management.

PREVENTION TECHNIQUES

- Set production goals by division and product line to meet customer needs.
- Formulate efficient purchase procedures.
- Implement engineering changes in production facilities quickly.
- Define production responsibility and lines of authority.
- Standardize inventory parts and production procedures where possible.
- Adjust salaries and increase employee benefits where necessary.
- Ask production personnel and shop supervisors for suggestions on how to improve manufacturing procedures.
- Establish that materials in inventory are available and properly identified.
- Institute quick materials inspection and rejection procedures for all receiving departments.

• Ensure that vendors are paid on time so that they will respond quickly to future purchase requests.
• Establish procedures for protecting inventory from theft.

SPILLOVER EFFECTS

• Inventory stockouts.
• Inability to meet customer sales.
• Increased insurance, storage, and administrative costs.
• Decline in net earnings.

See also in this chapter: HIGH RATE OF PRODUCT OBSOLESCENCE, INACCURATE INVENTORY RECORDS, *and* LOW TURNOVER OF MERCHANDISE.

PROBLEM
POOR-QUALITY GOODS
SYMPTOMS

• Excessive returns of merchandise.
• Discounts given to customers to keep goods.
• Declining sales and market share.
• A reputation for shoddy quality and workmanship.

CAUSES

• Obsolete production facilities.
• New, inexperienced, or unproductive workers.
• Poor-quality materials.
• Scheduling problems.
• Cutting corners on materials and workmanship.
• Failure to inspect materials before they are introduced into the manufacturing process.
• Poor quality control and lack of inspection procedures.
• Substitution of improper parts.
• Ignorance or violation of federal, state, and local regulations governing product safety standards.
• Failure to investigate consumer complaints.
• Improper packaging of goods that allows products to be damaged in transit to customers.

- Mislabeling of goods, causing customers to expect a better-quality product than the item actually purchased.
- Arrogance or complacency toward buyers.

ANALYSIS

- Look for trends in the ratio of sales returns and allowances to sales. An increasing trend indicates quality problems and unhappy customers.
- Compare returns to industry norms and those of competing companies.
- Appoint a group familiar with the manufacturing operations to advise top management on quality control.
- Set quality control standards.
- Evaluate the product inspection process.
- Review packaging techniques.

REPAIR

- Diagnose any weaknesses in each sector of the company associated with the production process.
- Evaluate the performance of production managers, supervisors, and workers.
- Formulate and publicize a policy of quality control.
- Inspect goods at key points during processing.
- Establish a program to replenish stocks of parts if they fall below a certain level.
- Update any obsolete production facilities.
- Retrain and motivate workers to produce quality work.·
- Change suppliers if any raw materials are inferior or contain an inordinate number of defects.
- Set reasonable production timetables.
- Do not allow corners to be cut on materials and workmanship.
- Inspect raw materials before they are introduced into the manufacturing process.
- Seek the advice of legal counsel and product engineers about safety standards the product must meet.
- Respond promptly to consumer complaints.
- Redesign the packaging of goods to avoid damage in transit.
- If necessary, select a new delivery company.

• Change any misleading labels on goods.
• Discontinue products considered of low quality or unreliable.
• Create and promote products that offer high quality and reliability at an affordable price.

PREVENTION TECHNIQUES

• Review production proficiency and quality control every three months, appraising everything from organizational structure and production objectives to inventory control methods.
• Evaluate the performance of all personnel associated with production.
• Establish a committee to review consumer complaints.
• Redesign packaging.
• Monitor the performance of the delivery company for customer complaints about goods damaged in transit.
• Hire product engineers to review safety standards in the product manufacturing process.
• Standardize labels.
• Mount an advertising campaign to improve the image of the product in the minds of the consuming public.
• Make all employees aware that consumer approval of the company's products is vital to the company's economic survival.

SPILLOVER EFFECTS

Poor-quality goods will cause sales and net earnings to decline and seriously damage the company's image. Competitors will take away market share. Violating product safety standards can lead to government intervention and high legal costs.
See also in this chapter: HIGH RATE OF PRODUCT OBSOLESCENCE, INACCURATE INVENTORY RECORDS, *and* LOW TURNOVER OF MERCHANDISE.

PROBLEM
LACK OF STORAGE SPACE

SYMPTOMS

- Missed production deadlines.
- Missing parts.
- Theft and damage to inventory.
- Storage space far from production facilities, resulting in delays and excessive transportation and handling costs.

CAUSES

- Incorrect sales forecasts.
- Improper production planning.
- Obsolete facilities.
- Lack of money to buy or build additional storage facilities.
- Rental storage space unavailable.
- High rental cost of storage space.
- Failure to assign managerial responsibility for control and storage of inventory.

ANALYSIS

- Prepare a forecast of storage requirements based on production schedules.
- Analyze storage bottlenecks, how materials are transported from storage areas to the production line, the distance they have to travel, and their weight and size.
- Study how the inventory is protected while in storage.
- Ascertain the frequency of emergency customer orders, so that just enough extra inventory can be kept on hand.
- Calculate the storage space needed to accommodate production schedules.

REPAIR

- Document the physical characteristics of the warehouse facilities.
- Determine the quantity and effective capacity of storage containers and bins currently in use.
- Make a detailed layout of the storage facilities, noting all movable and immovable objects.

- Observe how storeroom employees stock and pull goods.
- Investigate access to and security of storage areas.
- Identify any problems in the handling of goods.
- Determine how much of the inventory is obsolete or damaged and dispose of it at once to create additional storage space.
- Assign managerial responsibility for the control and storage of inventory.

PREVENTION TECHNIQUES

- For smaller parts buy adjustable shelves that slide on floor rollers to save space.
- Install carousel-type racks to lessen square-footage space requirements.
- Use open space at the top of the room by installing taller racks.
- Standardize package sizes.
- Rent storage space positioned to best serve consumer markets.
- Stock products at locations that promote efficiency in handling.
- Determine the proper level for all inventory parts and set up a computer system that gives immediate warning of both understand overstocking.
- Set up procedures to prevent damage to or loss of the inventory.

SPILLOVER EFFECTS

Insufficient storage space will create materials shortages, production downtime, inventory stockouts, theft opportunities, and an inability to meet emergency customer orders. These problems will cause a decline in sales and in net earnings.

See also in this chapter: INACCURATE INVENTORY RECORDS.

PROBLEM
DELAYED RECEIPT OF NEW INVENTORY

SYMPTOMS

- Lack of critical information related to production requirements.
- Continuous stockouts, shortages of materials, and missed production goals.
- Costs for placing inventory orders that are above the industry averages.

• Lack of management knowledge of the type and quantity of materials held at company storage sites, causing confusion and materials shortages at key areas.

CAUSES

• An inadequate inventory distribution system.
• Untrained or inexperienced personnel.
• Poor interface between manufacturing and purchase order systems.
• Generation of irrelevant and confusing information regarding purchase requirements.
• Problems with suppliers.
• Lost or ambiguous orders.

ANALYSIS

• Analyze the efficiency of the current purchase system.
• Assign and document managerial responsibility for acquiring and inspecting goods.
• Determine which suppliers are most honest and reliable.
• Establish when specific items of inventory must be reordered.

REPAIR

• Design and install a new inventory acquisition system.
• Reduce the number of employees involved in reordering to prevent overlapping functions.
• Train current employees in correct purchase methodology.
• Select the best suppliers. Eliminate vendors who ship damaged inventory or fail to deliver on time.
• Select suppliers close to the manufacturing facilities to promote quick delivery of goods ordered.
• Set up a system for soliciting bids that obtains the goods quickly at the best prices.
• Analyze all inventory parts according to predetermined usage life. Use the data to set up a system of automatic reordering.
• Study shipment procedures to determine which shipping companies deliver ordered goods on time.
• Renegotiate contracts with suppliers to penalize them for late deliveries.

PREVENTION TECHNIQUES

- Install a purchasing structure that uses the EOQ system.
- Maintain a computerized database for all inventory parts. Use it to standardize ordering requirements, amounts usually ordered, and average life for all materials during an average production period.
- Where feasible, implement a computerized purchasing system that automatically requests supplies of parts when units on hand fall below a specific amount. Consolidate all similar goods at one location to promote efficient reordering.
- Assign employee responsibilities for purchases. An updated purchasing system should reduce inventory-related paperwork, facilitate coordinated purchasing, reduce the time it takes to receive goods ordered, and improve communication among all company personnel involved in production.
- Give vendors a list of trucking companies considered reliable and demand that these companies be used for shipping orders to the company.

SPILLOVER EFFECTS

Delayed receipt of new inventory will cause scheduling problems in manufacturing, as well as inventory stockouts, inability to meet customer sales requests, production downtime, and declining sales. Net earnings will decline.

See also in this chapter: INACCURATE INVENTORY RECORDS, LOW TURNOVER OF MERCHANDISE *and* POOR-QUALITY GOODS.

Chapter 4
Weak Profit and Contribution Margin

A company must break even on its products and services to avoid losses. Breaking even simply means that total revenue equals total cost. Profit is zero.

Losses may arise when costs are excessive relative to production volume. Cost controls may be needed. There may also be a poor sales mix in the product or service line. Unprofitable business segments drain earnings and corporate resources. A loss on even one contract can have a devastating effect on the bottom line. Modifying or refining a product should never have adverse consequences on quantity, quality, or profitability.

In this chapter, we examine the following problems:

• Unrealistic breakeven point.
• Product or service failing to break even.
• Excessive cost given production volume.
• Weak sales mix.
• Unprofitable profit centers.
• Potential loss of a contract.
• Product refinement that generates a loss.

PROBLEM
UNREALISTIC BREAKEVEN POINT

SYMPTOM

The breakeven number calculated is much higher or lower than expected.

CAUSE

A faulty breakeven point is due to a fixed cost or contribution margin that is either higher or lower than is realistic.

ANALYSIS

The guidelines for breaking even dictate that an increase in selling price lowers the sales needed to break even, and increases in either variable or fixed costs increases them. One way to determine whether the breakeven point is realistic is to calculate the margin of safety (the difference between actual sales and breakeven sales). The margin of safety is the amount by which sales revenue may drop before losses begin. It is expressed as a percentage of expected sales:

$$\text{Margin of safety} = \frac{\text{Expected sales - Breakeven sales}}{\text{Expected sales}}$$

The margin of safety is used to measure operating risk. The larger the ratio, the safer the situation because there is less risk of falling to the breakeven point.

Breakeven Analysis. The givens of breakeven analysis are these:
- The selling price is constant, which in turn requires the following assumptions:

  Elasticity of demand is very high if the selling price remains the same when sales volume increases. (Demand elasticity refers to percentage change in product demand relative to percentage change in price.) The selling price is stable over the income period.
- There is only one product or a constant sales mix.
- Manufacturing efficiency is constant.
- Inventories do not materially change from period to period.
- The variable cost per unit is constant. (A variable cost is one that varies with volume, such as materials.)

- Total fixed cost is constant. (A fixed cost is one that remains constant regardless of activity, such as rent and insurance.)
- Fixed and variable costs are properly segregated

   Example: Porter Toy Stores projects sales of $35,000 with the breakeven point at $25,000. The projected margin of safety is:

$$\frac{\$35,000 - \$25,000}{\$35,000} = 28.75\%.$$

Cash breakeven point. If a company has minimal cash available or if the opportunity cost of holding excess cash is high, the enterprise may want to determine the sales volume needed to cover all cash expenses during a period. Note that not all fixed costs require cash payment (depreciation expense is an example). *What to do:* To find the cash breakeven point, reduce fixed costs by the noncash charges. The cash breakeven point will thus be less than the general breakeven point.

   Example: The selling price of a unit is $40, the variable cost unit is $10, and the fixed cost is $64,000 (including depreciation of $4,000). The number of units that must be sold to break even is:

$$\frac{\text{Fixed costs - Depreciation}}{\text{Contribution margin per unit}} = \frac{\$64,000 - \$4,000}{\$40 - \$10} = \frac{\$60\ 000}{\$30} = 2,000 \text{ units}$$

REPAIR

Recalculate the breakeven numbers obtained in the analysis section. If the calculated values do not match current values, correct the product values to get a proper breakeven.

PREVENTION TECHNIQUES

Reaffirm the company's fixed cost and contribution margin before calculating the breakeven point.

SPILLOVER EFFECTS

If the price of a product is too low, profits may decline. If it is too high, sales may fall. Declining profits from falling sales may adversely affect the company's stock price, bond offerings, market share, cost of financing, and ability to maintain future operations. Costs will have to be reduced, requiring the elimination of certain nonessential (and perhaps essential) operations and personnel. An unprofitable company will be forced to lay off workers. The possibility of insolvency and bankruptcy may also increase.

See also in this chapter PRODUCT OR SERVICE FAILING TO BREAK EVEN, POOR-QUALITY EARNINGS, *and* REVENUE BASE EROSION.

PROBLEM
PRODUCT OR SERVICE FAILING TO BREAK EVEN

SYMPTOMS

- The product or service is not generating a profit.
- Earnings are decreasing though sales are increasing. (At the cal- culated breakeven point, the company should show zero profit/zero loss for the product.)
- The company shows a financial loss on the product at any point in its life.

CAUSES

- Excessive production costs.
- A selling price that does not yield enough profit.
- Production quantities that are too high or too low.
- Poor general economic conditions, causing lower customer demand for the product or service.
- An unprofitable product mix. A product line that has a high positive correlation among products on the same line puts the company at great risk, since the demand for all the products moves in the same direction. Further, products with elastic demand can experience sig- nificant changes in quantity sold with only modest changes in price.
- A high debt structure, which means high fixed interest charges.
- A product that is highly price elastic, so an increase in selling price results in a sharp decline in profits.
- Reduced sales of a product that brings units sold below the expect- ed breakeven point.

• A product with a higher variable cost than was initially calculated.

ANALYSIS

Cost-volume-profit analysis relates to how profit and costs change with a change in production volume. As an aid to planning, it examines the impact on earnings of changes in such factors as variable cost, fixed cost, selling price, volume, and product mix. Breakeven analysis is useful when starting a new project, expanding a project, or downsizing a project.

A company's business objective is not to break even but to earn a profit. An enterprise can extend breakeven analysis to concentrate on a desired earnings figure. To compute the breakeven point, we consider fixed cost (FC) and variable cost (VC) along with the following important concepts:

• *Contribution margin (CM).* The contribution margin is the excess of sales (S) over VC for a product or service. It is the amount of money available to cover FC and generate profit. Symbolically, CM = S - VC.

• *Unit CM.* The unit CM is the excess of the unit selling price (p) over the unit variable cost (v). Symbolically, unit CM = p - v.

• *CM ratio.* The CM ratio is the contribution margin as a percentage of sales:

The CM ratio can also be computed using per-unit data:

$$\text{CM ratio} = \frac{CM}{S} = \frac{S\text{-}VC}{S} = 1 - \frac{VC}{S}$$

$$\text{CM ratio} = \frac{\text{Unit CM}}{p} = \frac{p\text{-}v}{p} = 1 - \frac{p}{v}$$

Note that the CM ratio is 1 minus the variable cost ratio. For example, if variable costs account for 70 percent of the price, the CM ratio is 30 percent.

Example 1: To illustrate the various CM concepts and calculate the breakeven point, consider the data shown in Table 4.1 for Porter Toy Stores.

Using the data in the table, CM, unit CM, and the CM ratio are computed as:

CM = S - VC = $37,500 - $15,000 = $22,500.

Unit CM = p − v = $25 -$10 = $15.

$$\text{CM ratio} = \frac{\text{CM}}{\text{S}} = \frac{\$22,500}{37,500} = 60\% \text{ or } \frac{\text{Unit CM}}{\text{P}} = \frac{\$15}{\$25} = 0.6 = 60\%$$

TABLE 4.1. CALCULATING BREAKEVEN

	Total	*Per Unit*	*Percentage*
Sales (1500 units)	$37,500	$25	100%
Less: Variable costs	$15,000	$10	40%
Contribution margin	$22,500	$15	60%
Less: Fixed costs	$15,000		
Net income	$ 7,500		

The Breakeven point is the level of sales revenue that equals the total of variable and fixed costs for a given volume of output at a particular capacity use rate. For example, management might want to calculate the Breakeven occupancy (or vacancy) rate for a hotel or the Breakeven load rate for an airliner.

Generally, other things being equal, the higher the Breakeven point the lower the profit and the greater the operating risk. The Breakeven point gives financial managers insights into profit planning. It can be computed using the following formulas:

$$\text{Breakeven point in units} = \frac{\text{Fixed costs}}{\text{Unit CM}}$$

$$\text{Breakeven point in dollars} = \frac{\text{Fixed costs}}{\text{Unit CM}}$$

Example 2: Using the data given in Example 1, where unit CM = $25 - $10 = $15 and CM ratio = 60%, we get:

Breakeven point in units = $15,000/$15 = 1,000 units.

Breakeven point in dollars = $15,000/0.6 = $25,000.

Or, alternatively,

1,000 units x $25 = $25,000.

Example 3: A manager is thinking of making a product that is currently bought from outside suppliers for $0.12 per unit. The fixed cost of the production machinery is $10,000, and the variable cost per unit is $0.08. The number of units that have to be sold or used so that the annual cost of the machine equals the outside purchase cost is:

$$\frac{\text{Fixed costs}}{\text{CM per unit}} = \frac{\$10,000}{\$0.12 - \$0.08} = \frac{\$10,000}{\$0.04} = \$250,000 \text{ units.}$$

Example 4: A company wants to determine how many units it must sell to make after-tax profits. Assume the following:

Selling price	= $40
Variable cost	= $24
Fixed cost	= $150,000
After-tax profit	= $240,000
Tax rate	= 40%

$$\text{Desired units} = \frac{\text{Fixed costs} + \text{Before - tax profit}}{\text{Contribution margin (CM) per unit}}$$

$$\frac{\$150,000 + \$400,000}{\$40 - \$24} = \frac{\$550,000}{\$16} = 34,375 \text{ units}$$

$$0.6 \text{ x before - tax profit} = \$240,000;$$
$$\text{so before - tax profit} = \frac{\$240,000}{0.6} = \$400,000$$

Sales mix. Breakeven analysis requires more computations when more than one product is produced and sold. Different selling prices and different variable costs can result in different contribution margins. As a consequence, breakeven points for the whole company can change depending on the sales mix, the proportions of each product sold. An assumption in breakeven analysis for a multiproduct business is that the sales mix will not change during the planning period. If it does, the breakeven point will also change.

REPAIR

- Reduce long-term debt.
- Refinance debt at low interest rates.
- Cut down discretionary fixed costs, such as those for advertising, research and development, training, and public relations.
- Trim the labor force.
- Downsize operations and sell off marginal assets and profit centers.
- Reduce variable costs.
- Find less costly combinations of raw materials.
- Use JIT techniques to reduce the breakeven point.

- Improve the efficiency of the production line by reducing labor costs for manufacturing the product.

PREVENTION TECHNIQUES

- Tightly control all costs.
- Use surplus funds to pay off or reduce debt.
- Use statistical cost control charts to ensure that the cost stays within a normal (tolerable) range.
- Introduce new products using JIT supply chains.
- Reconfirm the breakeven point of the product before it enters the market and if necessary adjust the price.

SPILLOVER EFFECTS

Continuous deterioration in profits would lower the market value of the company. When a product or service does not break even, it generates losses, and in the long run the company may be forced to shut down. Even if the company survives, its failure to break even may prevent it from introducing new products or services, modernizing its facilities, and heading off production and administrative problems.

See also in this chapter: UNREALISTIC BREAK-EVEN POINT. *In Chapter 6*: EXCESSIVE OPERATING LEVERAGE

PROBLEM
EXCESSIVE COST-TO-PRODUCTION VOLUME

SYMPTOMS

- Sales result in low or no profits even if all the items produced are sold at a fair market price.
- As production volume increases, so do losses.
- The product does not show a profit at the expected breakeven point.

CAUSES

- The production volume is too low or too high. If actual production is below optimum, opportunity cost (the cost of not producing more to make additional profits) is added to total manufacturing cost. Hence the cost for the production volume would be too high. If actual production volume is too high, excess production is not sold and becomes a sunk cost that increases total manufacturing cost. (A sunk cost is one incurred in the past that will not be affected by any decision made now or in the future.) The result again is that the cost for the production volume will be too high.

- The company is unable to control or cut down on costs.
- Managers do not understand the relationship between cost and production volume.
- There is no cost-control system, such as the use of variance analysis (comparing actual to standard cost) and statistical cost control.
- The breakeven point calculated in early production runs was unrealistic.
- The cost of the product has increased since the original value was calculated.
- Yields of the product are lower than predicted, thus increasing cost.

ANALYSIS

- Use the CM ratio (contribution margin/sales) to help determine whether variable costs are too high. Compare the ratio with the industry average to make that decision, and perform a contribution analysis. *See Chapter 11:* MARGINS SHRUNK BY LOWERED PRICES.
- Use the earnings before interest and taxes (EBIT) over sales ratio to determine whether fixed costs are too high for the production volume, assuming the CM is normal.
- Plot costs over time to see if they are out of the ordinary. Examine the trend in the relationship between cost and production volume.
- Measure unit cost for each product affected. If the result is higher than initially targeted, look for production problems.
- Measure yields of the product. The yields should be at or above predetermined values to meet cost projections.
- Analyze the productivity and efficiency of each department.

REPAIR

- Reduce operating costs.
- Identify desired levels of productivity and efficiency department or unit.
- Cut nonessential expenditures, though not vital operating costs. Some possible solutions in each area are as follows:

Payroll:

- Look for overstaffing in every functional area.
- Reduce excess personnel and terminate those whose performance is less than satisfactory.

Manufacturing:

- Use computer-aided product design and manufacturing.
- Work to reduce high levels of scrap, defective work, rework, and customer returns.
- Consider JIT inventory planning.
- Investigate causes of labor and machine downtime.
- Establish employee training programs to increase worker productivity.
- Reduce the cycle time for production. A reduction in cycle time reduces work-in-process (WIP) and the accompanying costs.

PREVENTION TECHNIQUES

- Draw up a schedule showing the different capacities at which the firm can produce products.
- Calculate accurate costs for producing each item.
- Find a good equilibrium price. This, together with accurate analysis of both production capacity and costs, will help determine the number of units that need to be produced to maximize profits.
- Institute techniques to lower cost before starting production.
- Go over variable costs again before start-up to determine whether they are still valid.

SPILLOVER EFFECTS

Excessive costs relative to manufacturing volume may result in planning and scheduling inefficiencies, cancellation of contracts, and reduction of staff. Excessive cost-to-production-volume leads to high opportunity and sunk costs that can reduce profits to zero. If that happens, earnings per share go down, and so does the price of the stock. The company may also have to accept a lower issuance price for its bonds, which will raise the cost of financing to compensate for the increased risk of lower profits. Increasing sales prices to recoup losses may cause a loss of business.

See also in this chapter: PRODUCT OR SERVICE NOT BREAKING EVEN *and* UNREALISTIC BREAKEVEN POINT. *In Chapter 6:* DISTORTED COST INFORMATION, EXCESSIVE LABOR COSTS *and* INADEQUATE COST CONTROLS. *In Chapter 12:* COSTS NOT CLOSELY TRACKED.

PROBLEM
WEAK SALES MIX
SYMPTOMS

- Sales mix is not as budgeted.
- Lower-priced products are sold at a disproportionately high rate compared to higher-priced, higher-margin items.
- There is excessive inventory of one product.
- Costs are higher than originally budgeted.

CAUSES

- It is often easier to sell lower-margin (cheaper) items than top-of-the-line models.
- Sales quotas are set in number of units to be sold rather than in profits to be made.
- There is a shift in sales mix toward a less profitable product line.
- The cost of a product increases above its projected sales value.

ANALYSIS

Compute the profitability for each product.

Example: Dante, Inc. is a producer of recreational equipment. It expects to produce and sell three types of sleeping bags (1) the Economy, (2) the Regular, and (3) the Backpacker. Information on the bags is given in Table 4.2.

TABLE 4.2. PROJECTED SALES MIX FOR SLEEPING BAGS
Budgeted

	Economy	Regular	Backpacker	T
Sales	$30,000	$60,000	$10,000	$100,000
Sales mix	30%	60%	10%	100%
Less: Variable costs (VC)	24,000	40,000	5,000	69,000
Contribution margin (CM)	$6,000	$20,000	$5,000	$31,000
CM ratio	20%	33 1/3%	50%	31%
Fixed costs				$ 18,600
Net income				$ 12,400

Total sales were indeed $100,000 but the actual sales mix was not as budgeted. The differences are shown in Table 4.3.

TABLE 4.3. ACTUAL SALES MIX FOR SLEEPING BAGS
Actual

	Economy	Regular	Backpacker	Total
Sales	$55,000	40,000	$5,000	$100,000
Sales mix	55%	40%	5%	100%
Less: Variable costs (VC)	44,000	26,667 *	2500 **	73,167
Contribution margin (CM)	$11,000	$13,333	$52,500	$26,833
CM ratio	20%	33 1/3%	50%	26.83%
Fixed costs				$ 18,600
Net income				$ 8,233

*$26,667 = $40,000 x (100% - 33 1/3%) = $40,000 x 66 2/3%.
**$2,500 = $5,000 x (100% - 50%) = $5,000 x 50%.

The shift in sales mix toward the less profitable Economy line caused the CM ratio for the company as a whole to drop from 31 percent to 26.83 percent. The deterioration in the mix caused net income to go down. If the mix had improved toward the more profitable lines, net income would have gone up. Generally, a shift of emphasis from low-margin to high-margin products will increase company profits.

REPAIR

- Reduce the price of slow-moving products to make them more competitive.
- Increase advertising of slow-moving products to help move the inventory.

• Increase advertising of higher-margin products to encourage their sales and increase profits.

Many product lines have both a lower-margin price leader and a high-margin deluxe model. To increase profitability, management may want to emphasize the higher-margin expensive items while the sales force finds it easier to sell the cheaper models. Thus, a salesperson might meet the unit sales quota with each item at its budgeted price, but because of mix shifts could be far short of contributing an appropriate share of budgeted profit. Management must realize that selling more of more profitable products means higher profits. Selling more of low-margin products reduces profit despite the increase in sales volume. Thus, an unfavorable mix may easily offset a favorable increase in volume, and vice versa.

PREVENTION TECHNIQUES

• Motivate the sales force to sell higher-CM lines by setting profit quotas rather than quotas of units sold.
• Price products competitively.
• Advertise products early in the production cycle to create a strong market for them.
• Create a need for the product in the market.

SPILLOVER EFFECTS

Insufficient sales of high CM lines in favor of lower-margin items will lead to an inventory buildup of higher-cost finished goods; a need to sell more units, increasing the marketing costs; and a shift in the production mix toward lower-margin items. A poor sales mix may ultimately cause loss of revenue and decline in profitability. There could even be a temporary stoppage of production for the product. If production stops, inventory doesn't build, it just sits there. Such a shutdown might necessitate the layoff of employees until production resumes.

See Chapter 11: REVENUE BASE EROSION.

PROBLEM
UNPROFITABLE PROFIT CENTERS
SYMPTOM

A profit center (a segment of a business that is evaluated on the profit it earns) generates a financial loss each month.

CAUSES

* A particular segment, or group of segments, of a firm is failing to generate sufficient CM to cover direct fixed costs plus allocated common fixed costs.
* A transfer price is the price charged by one department for an internal transfer of an assembled product or service to another department. In a transfer-pricing situation, the selling division may not be receiving enough credit for the value of the goods and services it transfers to the buying division, so its actual positive operating performance is distorted.

ANALYSIS

It is necessary to do segmental reporting of financial performance by department, based on the contribution approach. A typical format for a CM report evaluating the performance of the division and its manager is:

Sales ... *Less* Variable production cost of sales
Equals Manufacturing contribution margin
Less Variable selling and administrative expenses
Equals CM
Less Controllable fixed costs (e.g., salesperson salaries)
Equals Controllable CM by manager (which measures
the performance of the segment as well as the manager)
Less Uncontrollable fixed costs (e.g., depreciation, property taxes, insurance)
Equals Segment CM (performance of the division)
Less Unallocated costs to divisions (some costs are excessively difficult to allocate objectively or are illogical to allocate, such as the president's salary and corporate research)
Equals Income before taxes (performance of the company in its entirety).

Contribution reporting of this type is based on the following three assumptions:

1. Fixed costs are much less controllable than variable costs.
2. Direct fixed costs and common fixed costs must be ditinguished. Direct fixed costs are those that can be allocated directly to a particular segment of an organization. Common fixed costs are those that cannot because they apply to the company as a whole.
3. Common fixed costs should be clearly identified as unallocated in the contribution income statement by segments. Any attempt to allocate these types of costs on some arbitrary basis can destroy the value of responsibility accounting. It would lead to unfair evaluation of performance and misleading managerial decisions.

The following concepts are highlighted in the contribution approach:

- Contribution margin equals sales minus variable costs.
- Segment margin equals contribution margin minus direct (traceable) fixed costs. Direct fixed costs include discretionary costs like advertising and research and development; sales promotion; engineering; and committed costs like depreciation, property taxes, insurance, and segment manager salaries.
- Net income equals segment margin less unallocated common fixed costs. Segmental reporting can be made by division, product or product line, sales territory, service center, salesperson, store or branch office, or domestic or foreign operation.

The margin is the best measure of the profitability of a segment. No attempt should be made to apportion unallocated fixed costs in order not to distort the performance results of segments.

When the profit center is a product or service, it is important to analyze operating performance to determine if the product should be kept or dropped. The same kind of contribution approach can be used.

The decision about whether or not to drop a product line must take into account both qualitative and quantitative factors. However, any final decision should be based primarily on how the decision will affect CM contribution margin or net income.

Example: Tasty Food Corporation has three major product lines:

produce, meats, and canned food. The company is thinking about dropping the meat line because the income statement shows that it is being sold at a loss. The income statement for these product lines is shown in Table 4.4.

TABLE 4.4. COMPARISON OF PRODUCT LINE PROFITABILITY

	Produce	*Meats*	*Canned Food*	*Total*
Sales	$10,000	$15,000	$25,000	$50,000
Less variable costs	6,000	8,000	12,000	26,000
Contribution margin (CM)	$4,000	$7,000	$13,000	$24,000
Less fixed costs				
Direct	$2,000	$6,500	$4,000	$12,500
Allocated	1,000	1,500	2,500	5,000
Total	$3,000	$8,000	$6,500	$ 17,500
Net income	$1,000	$(1,000)	$6,500	$6,500

The direct fixed costs shown in the table are those that are identified directly with each product lines. Allocated fixed costs are the amount of common fixed costs allocated to the product lines using some base, such as space occupied. The common fixed costs typically continue and thus cannot be saved by dropping the product line.

The comparative approach showing the effects on the company as a whole with and without the meat line is shown in Table 4.5.

TABLE 4.5. EFFECT OF DROPPING A PRODUCT LINE

	Keep Meats	*Drop Meats*	*Difference*
Sales	$50,000	$35,000	$(15,000)
Less variable costs	26,000	18,000	(5,000)
Contribution margin (CM)	$24,000	$17,000	$(7,000)
Less fixed costs			
Direct	$12,500	$6,000	$(6,500)
Allocated	5,000	5,000	–
Total	$17,500	$11,000	$(6,500)
Net income	$6,500	$6,000	$(500)

One of the great dangers in allocating common fixed costs is that such allocations can make a product line look less profitable than it really is. Because of that allocation, the meat line showed a loss of $1,000, but in effect it contributes $500 ($7000 - $6500) to the recovery of the company's common fixed costs. From the table, we see that because by dropping the meat line the company will lose an additional $500, the line should be kept.

All arbitrary allocations of overhead should be ignored when a segment's performance is evaluated. In deciding whether to discontinue operations, it is necessary to consider the direct (removable) fixed costs, the CM, and the bottom line effect on the firm's profitability.

REPAIR

Sell or liquidate unprofitable profit centers if the CM is negative, but a "what if" analysis is required to ascertain whether divestiture would improve the performance of the firm as a whole.

PREVENTION TECHNIQUES

Reorganize the profit center and provide stronger management to improve cost and yields.

SPILLOVER EFFECTS

Depending on the extent of the loss, retaining unprofitable profit centers can drive down profits or it can maintain higher profits (if the CM is positive). In a drive-down situation, staff may have to be reduced to cut costs. Elimination of a product may cause customers for other products in the line to find an alternate supplier, resulting in lost business for the company. Failure to eliminate or correct unprofitable business segments may ultimately result in lower credit ratings, decline in the market price of the company's stocks and bonds, and in severe cases insolvency and bankruptcy.

See in Chapter 5: LACK OF RESIDUAL INCOME *and* LOW RATE OF RETURN. *In Chapter 6*: LACK OF COST INFORMATION *and* EXCESSIVE LABOR COSTS. *In Chapter 9:* ACTUAL COSTS EXCEEDING BUDGETED COSTS. *In Chapter 13*: INABILITY TO CURB FINANCIAL PROBLEMS.

PROBLEM
POTENTIAL LOSS OF A CONTRACT

SYMPTOMS

- Friction between company and client.
- Disagreements over as pricing, quality, and timely delivery.
- Customer refusal to pay and threats of lawsuits for breach of contract.
- Competitors offering to sell the merchandise or service contracted for at a lower price.

CAUSES

- The company cannot manufacture the product or deliver the service because it lacks expertise or has labor problems.
- Government contracts have become uncertain because of cuts in spending and changes in priorities.
- Prices have not been computed correctly.
- Quality control is poor.
- Commitments made to clients cannot be met.
- Poor economic conditions lead to order cancellations.
- Other companies offer tough competition for the contract.
- The company lacks the facilities or expertise to deliver the product or service.

ANALYSIS

Pricing policies using CM analysis may be helpful in contract negotiations for a product or service. Often such business is sought during the slack season, when it may be financially beneficial to bid on extra business at a competitive price that at least covers all variable costs and makes some contribution to fixed costs plus profits. Knowledge of variable and fixed costs is necessary to make an accurate price bid.

REPAIR

- Determine the price to charge on a contract using relevant costing (costs relevant to a decision) when capacity is idle. At idle capacity, total fixed costs are irrelevant to pricing a contract. A contract may appear to be a loss because total costs (fixed and variable) exceed total revenue, but the contract should be accepted as long as there is a CM (total revenue exceeds variable cost) because profit is earned since incremental fixed costs are zero.

- Subcontract the work if the company lacks the proper production facilities or expertise to deliver the product or service.

For a fuller discussion, *see Chapter 11*: LOWERED PRICES SHRINKING MARGINS.

PREVENTION TECHNIQUES

- Expand inspections during production to assure that the product meets quality standards.
- Approve overtime and expand the staff to assure that the product or service is delivered on time.
- Keep the client up-to-date about unexpected, unavoidable bottle-necks.
- Discuss any production or financial problems with the client in a friendly manner and make compromises as needed.
- Engage in joint ventures with other companies to share possible risks.
- Establish a public relations program to protect current business and attract new business by emphasizing the positive attributes (reliability, integrity, quality of product or service) of the company. (If the situation is bad, a change in name may enable a company to divorce itself from its old negative reputation.)
- Examine all future contracts to ensure that the company does not overestimate its ability to deliver a product or service.

SPILLOVER EFFECTS

A loss of contracts means declines in revenue, profitability, and cash flow. Layoffs may be necessary, along with other cost reduction programs. Other sources of business reliant on those contracts may be lost. Clients who perceive the company as having problems may shift their business to competitors.

See also in this chapter: PRODUCT OR SERVICE FAILING TO BREAK EVEN. *In Chapter 6*: EXCESSIVE LABOR COSTS.

PROBLEM
LOSS RESULTING FROM
PRODUCT REFINEMENT

SYMPTOM

Falling sales or a narrowing profit margin.

CAUSES

Loss in sales or a shrinking profit margin may arise from:
- Cost overruns.
- Inaccurate pricing.
- Ineffective advertising.
- An overoptimistic estimate of demand for the product.

These may be the result of:
- Inadequate planning.
- Deficient engineering.
- Misstatement of cost estimates.
- Lack of product quality.
- Quantity of product offered at a given price.
- Production inefficiencies.
- Poor worker performance.

ANALYSIS

- Compare sales and profit before and after product refinement.
- Compare budgeted to actual costs.
- Analyze reasons for a change in product demand.

REPAIR

Determine whether data on direct labor and material costs are accurate.
If not, some management options are to:
- Stop production.
- Immediately increase the retail price of the product.
- Cut costs.
- Streamline the manufacturing process by changing plant layout.

Prevention Techniques
- Plan carefully before refining the product.
- Separate all factory and corporate support systems and trace them to individual products being offered for sale.
- Reduce the costs of logistics, production, marketing and sales, distribution, product services, technology, and financial and general administration.
- Ask the accounting department to provide realistic cost figures related to the change.
- Train workers in the modified product.
- Use customer surveys to determine whether there is a demand for the proposed refined product.
- Test-market the product before it is introduced.
- Set up a separate company with a different name to protect the parent company from failure.
- Increase product liability insurance against possible consumer lawsuits based on negligent manufacture of the product.

SPILLOVER EFFECTS

A refined product that is not profitable will lower earnings and risk customer dissatisfaction that can cost the firm future sales. The product may also generate government investigation because of possible deceptive practices.

Chapter 5
Anemic Financial Statements

A business that fails to maintain adequate liquid assets cannot pay its obligations when due. This may lead to insolvency and possible bankruptcy. A company that owes more than it owns is in a very precarious financial situation. Its credit rating will deteriorate, resulting in less liquidity, higher costs of financing, lower prices for its stocks and bonds, and greater restrictions on the loans it does get. Suppliers will be reluctant to grant credit.

If assets are not used efficiently, profit margins will deteriorate and obsolescence may occur. A business can only regress when it is earning a low return on invested capital (total assets). High-risk assets cannot easily be sold to generate sufficient cash.

A declining trend in earnings coupled with low-quality elements on the income statement should raise a red flag of warning. Poor-quality earnings will result in a lower PE ratio, a lower bond rating, and excessive debt restrictions. Instability in operations means uncertainty and risk to investors, creditors, and suppliers. It is difficult to reliably predict future results when revenue and earnings trends are inconsistent.

The problems covered in this chapter are:
- Inadequate working capital.
- Inadequate liquidity.
- Insolvency.

- Excessive debt.
- Off-balance sheet liabilities.
- Deficient asset utilization.
- Low rate of return.
- Lack of residual income.
- High cash-realization risk in assets.
- Poor profitability and growth.
- Poor-quality earnings.
- Instability in Operations and earnings.
- Unstable sources of income.
- Low P/E ratio.

PROBLEM
INADEQUATE WORKING CAPITAL

SYMPTOMS

- Not enough funds available to meet current obligations.
- Difficulty collecting notes and accounts receivable, converting short-term investments into cash, and obtaining credit from suppliers.

CAUSES

- Working capital is inadequate because the company is engaged in capital expansion or is in a highly capital-intensive sector.
- Lack of cash flow from operations results in insufficient liquid assets.
- The company is financing noncurrent assets with short-term debt, a questionable financing strategy because the debt will have to be paid back before cash is received from the sale of fixed assets.

ANALYSIS

Working capital—the excess of total current assets over total current liabilities—is a measure of a company's short-term liquidity. It is a margin of safety for meeting the cash demands of the business operating cycle.

The trade-off between return and risk must be considered. If funds move from fixed assets (e.g., plant and equipment) to current assets (e.g., inventory), liquidity risk is reduced. The company is better able to obtain short-term financing and has greater financial flexibility, because the business can better adjust current assets to changes in sales volume. However, the return on current assets is usually less than the return on fixed assets. The longer it takes to manufacture goods or to resell purchased goods, the greater the demand for working capital.

REPAIR

Additional working capital can be generated by increasing current assets and decreasing current liabilities. Therefore, money should be invested in current rather than in fixed assets. Financing should be by long-term rather than short-term debt.

PREVENTION TECHNIQUES

- Finance the purchase of fixed assets with long-term debt.
- Borrow funds long-term and retain them in cash or other current assets.

SPILLOVER EFFECTS

A poor working capital position means that the company is less liquid. This can result in higher financing costs and an inability to obtain financing.

See also in this chapter: INADEQUATE LIQUIDITY. *In Chapter 1:* INADEQUATE CASH POSITION.

PROBLEM
INADEQUATE LIQUIDITY

SYMPTOMS

- Inability to pay bills and other debt obligations on time.
- Inability to buy necessary inventory or assets.
- Difficulty in obtaining loans on favorable terms.
- Inability to obtain financing at all.
- Lower profitability.
- Inability to take cash discounts by making early payment.
- A deteriorating credit rating.

CAUSES

- Failure to expedite the collection of receivables and to reduce the lag between the time customers pay their bills and the time the checks are converted into cash.
- Overspending.
- Excessive debt.
- Poor management of current assets (cash, accounts receivable, and inventory).
- Failure to properly assess risk.

ANALYSIS

There are numerous ways to evaluate liquidity, including the following ratios and computations:

- *Current ratio* (current assets/current liabilities) and *quick ratio* (cash plus marketable securities plus accounts receivable/current liabilities). High ratios are needed when a company has difficulty borrowing on short notice. Note: Current assets that are pledged to secure long-term liabilities are not available to meet current debt.
- *Accounts receivable turnover* (credit sales/average accounts receivable) and *collection period* (360/accounts receivable turnover). The higher the turnover the better because that means the company is collecting from customers quickly. (However, an excessively high turnover might indicate that the company's credit policy is too stringent, with the company not tapping the potential for profit through sales to customers in higher-risk classes.) The collection period indicates how long it takes to collect from customers. A long collection period warns of danger that customer balances may become uncollectible. Compare the collection period to the due date. Prepare an aging schedule. On occasion, however, a longer collection period may be justified, such as when the business extends the credit terms in connection with the introduction of a new product.
- *Inventory turnover* (cost of goods sold/average inventory) and *age of inventory* (360 days/inventory turnover). The inventory turnover reveals how many times inventory is sold during the year. A decline in the turnover rate indicates an inventory buildup, overestimation of sales, a lack of balance in inven-

tory, or deficiencies in the product line or marketing effort. On occasion, however, a low turnover may be appropriate, such as when inventory levels rise in anticipation of rapidly rising prices (as in the case of oil). A high turnover rate may indicate inadequate inventory levels, which may lead to a loss in business. The age of the inventory is the number of days products are held before sale. If the holding period increases, there is the risk of inability to sell the asset and possible obsolescence. If the holding period decreases, it may represent underinvestment in inventory that can cause deficient customer service and lost sales.

- *Operating cycle* is the number of days from cash to inventory to accounts receivable to cash. It equals the collection period on accounts receivable plus the age of inventory. The operating cycle reveals how long cash is tied up in receivables and inventory. A long cycle means cash is less available to meet short-term obligations.

- *Working capital* is the reserve available to satisfy contingenciesand uncertainties. It is the excess of current assets over current liabilities. A high working capital balance is mandated if the business is unable to borrow on short notice.

- A *high sales to current assets* ratio indicates an inadequate amount of working capital. Current liabilities may be due and payable before inventories and receivables can be converted into cash.

- *Working capital provided from net income* is useful to see where the company stands. A company's liquid position is improved when net profits result in liquid funds.

- *Working capital provided from operations to total liabilities* indicates the degree to which internally generated cash flow is available to satisfy obligations.

- *Cash* plus *marketable securities to current liabilities* shows the immediate amount available to satisfy short-term debt.

- A *low cash* plus *marketable securities to working capital* ratio means less protection to short-term creditors because there are fewer assets available to meet debt coming due.

- The *cost of sales, operating expenses, and taxes to average total current assets* ratio is used to analyze the adequacy of current assets to satisfy ongoing business-related expenses.
- *Quick assets to the year's cash expenses* indicates the number of days of total operating expenses that highly liquid assets could support.
- The *ratios of fixed assets to short-term debt and short-term debt to long-term debt* can indicate whether current financial policies are dangerous. A company that finances long-term assets with short-term obligations may have a problem meeting payments as they come due, because the return from the fixed assets will not be realized before the maturity dates. The business will be vulnerable in a money-market squeeze.
- *Accounts payable to average daily purchases* reveals the number of days it takes for the business to pay creditors. It measures the extent to which accounts payable represent current rather than overdue obligations.
- Higher ratios of *current liabilities to total liabilities* and c*urrent liabilities to noncurrent liabilities* mean less liquidity because a greater proportion of total debt must be paid shortly.
- The *defensive interval* ratio indicates how long the business can operate on its liquid assets without needing revenues from the next period. It reveals corporate near-term liquidity.
- The *liquidity index* indicates the number of days during which assets are removed as cash equivalents. It is computed as shown in Table 5.1.

TABLE 5.1. LIQUIDITY INDEX COMPUTATION

	Amounts	X	Days from Cash	=	Total
Cash	$20,000	X	—		—
Accounts receivable	50,000	X	30		$1,500,000
Inventory	80,000	X	50		4,000,000
	$150,000				$5,500,000
Index =	$5,550,000				
	150,000				
=	36.7 days				

A company's liquidity ratio should be comparable to industry norms and ratios of major competitors.

REPAIR

- Expedite collection of cash by reducing the lag between the time customers receive their bills and the time they actually pay.
- Delay disbursements so that the company can continue to use the cash.
- Convert investments into cash.
- Sell unprofitable operating divisions and subsidiaries.
- Open new credit lines.

PREVENTION TECHNIQUES

- Curb expenditures.
- Limit debt.
- Obtain lines of credit with financing institutions.
- Issue stocks or bonds.
- Restrict capital expansion.
- Slow cash disbursements to pay only impending obligations and invest excess funds.

SPILLOVER EFFECTS

- Inability to obtain short-term financing.
- Failure to meet payments on short-term debt.
- Lower credit rating.
- Decline in the market price of the company's stocks and bonds.
- Inability to make profitable investments.
- Possible insolvency and bankruptcy.

See also in this chapter: EXCESSIVE DEBT, INADEQUATE WORKING CAPITAL, *and* INSOLVENCY. *In Chapter 13:* BANKRUPTCY ON THE HORIZON.

PROBLEM
INSOLVENCY

SYMPTOMS

An insolvent business cannot meet its short- and long-term obligations
and make interest payments on time. This may be due to high fixed
interest costs, excessive debt, or both. There is also high risk of not
being able to realize noncurrent assets.

CAUSES

- Poor operating performance.
- Deficient cash flow.
- Liabilities in excess of the company's ability to pay.
- Debt incurred to prevent a hostile takeover.
- Managerial incompetence.

ANALYSIS

A company may be technically insolvent, even though its assets exceed
its liabilities, when it does not have sufficient liquid assets to pay maturing debts. The term bankruptcy indicates that liabilities exceed assets.
Under the law, either technical insolvency or bankruptcy is considered
financial failure of the company.

It is useful to study solvency ratios regularly and compare them to
industry averages. Some useful ratios are:

- *Total liabilities to stockholder equity* (commonly called the
  debt/equity ratio or *financial leverage*). High leverage is risky
  because it may be difficult for the company to pay interest and
  principal while trying to obtain additional financing. The ratio is
  more useful if securities are valued at their year-end market value
  rather than at book value.
- *Long-term debt* to *stockholder equity*. A higher ratio is unfavorable
  because it shows increased risk of being unable to repay long-term
  obligations.
- *Total liabilities to total assets* (commonly called the *debt ratio*). A
  high ratio is unfavorable because the company is already overbur-
  dened with debt.
- *Cash flow to long-term debt* appraises the adequacy of funds available to pay noncurrent obligations.

- *Net income before taxes* and *interest to interest* reflects the number of times interest expense is covered. It reveals the magnitude of the decline in income that a firm can absorb and still meet its interest payment obligations.
- *Cash flow generated from operations* plus *interest to interest* indicates the cash actually available to meet interest charges. It is cash, not net income, that is used to pay interest.
- *Net income before taxes* and *fixed charges to fixed charges* measures ability to meet fixed costs. The ratio indicates the risk when business activity falls and a company is in danger of being unable to pay its rent, insurance, and interest bills.
- *Cash flow provided from operations* plus *fixed charges to fixed charges* indicates the cash available to pay fixed charges.
- *Noncurrent assets to noncurrent liabilities.* Long-term debt will ultimately be paid out of long-term assets. A high ratio shows good protection for long-term creditors.
- *Retained earnings to total assets* reveals a company's profitability over the years.

REPAIR

- Sell marginal (unprofitable) assets.
- Close marginal operations.
- Restructure collection policies for credit sales.
- Obtain new credit lines.
- Sell corporate stock.
- Negotiate lengthened payment dates on obligations.
- Lay off employees.

PREVENTION TECHNIQUES

- Obtain additional financing from equity sources, such as by selling preferred and common stock.
- Negotiate open lines of credit.
- Shorten payback periods on projects.
- Adjust quickly to changes in business conditions.
- Change the amount and timing of future cash flows to be prepared for sudden developments.
- Downsize.
- Restructure.
- Practice conservative financial management.

SPILLOVER EFFECTS

Potential creditors are reluctant to give financing to a company with high debt. If they do make a loan, the interest rate will be higher. A company that cannot pay its creditors will be unable to operate effectively and profitably. It may face eventual bankruptcy.

See also in this chapter: EXCESSIVE DEBT *and* INADEQUATE LIQUIDITY. *In Chapter 13*: BANKRUPTCY ON THE HORIZON..

PROBLEM
EXCESSIVE DEBT

SYMPTOMS

- Cash flow problems.
- Loan restrictions.
- Lower credit rating.
- Inability to meet interest and principal payments on maturing debt.
- Increased financing costs.

CAUSES

- Interest and principal payment obligations set by contract must be met, regardless of changes in the company's economic position.
- Excessive debt is incurred to finance expansion or prevent a hostile takeover.
- A decline in profitability forces the company to borrow externally to finance operations.
- The business cannot issue additional shares of stock because prospective investors view it as a poor risk. It must issue debt securities or use lines of credit.
- Management has failed to realistically forecast business needs and cash flow.
- The company has not exercised fiscal self-control.
- Executives have failed to appreciate that growth at any cost may be too expensive.

ANALYSIS

Examine trends in the following ratios over the last five years:

- *Total debt to total stockholder equity.* A higher ratio means more debt and risk.
- *Noncurrent assets to noncurrent liabilities.* A lower ratio means fewer fixed assets are available to meet long-term debt.
- *Short-term debt to long-term debt.* A higher ratio means less liquidity because more debt is coming due in the short term.
- *Current liabilities to sales.* Short-term debt may have to be stretched to support sales growth.
- *Short-term debt to total liabilities.* A high ratio points to less liquidity.
- *Net income plus interest divided by interest.* A lower ratio means earnings are less available to meet interest payments.
- *Sales to accounts payable.* A high ratio indicates inability to obtain short-term credit in the form of cost-free funds to finance sales growth.

In appraising current liabilities, management must determine which liabilities are pressing and which are more patient. Patient liabilities (e.g., suppliers) are more tolerant. They may allow delayed payment or even adjust the amounts owed in times of financial difficulties. Pressing obligations like taxes and salaries, however, must be paid on time. Examine the trend in the relationship of pressing to patient liabilities. An increasing trend reflects greater liquidity risk.

Example: Company C reports the data shown in Table 5.2.

The higher ratios of current liabilities to total liabilities, current liabilities to sales, and pressing current liabilities to patient current liabilities mean that Company C has greater liquidity risk in 20X2.

Keep in mind off-balance-sheet liabilities that are not reported in the body of the financial statements but may require future payment or services, such as litigation, lease commitments, and cosigned loans.

TABLE 5.2. CURRENT LIABILITIES AND SALES RATIOS
FOR COMPANY C

	20X1	*20X2*
Current liabilities		
Accounts payable	$30,000	$26,000
Short-term loans payable	50,000	80,000
Commercial paper	40,000	60,000
Total current liabilities	$120,000	$166,000
Total noncurrent liabilities	300,000	302,000
Total liabilities	$420,000	$468,000
Sales	$1,000,000	$1,030,000
Ratios		
Current liabilities to total liabilities	28.6%	35.5%
Current liabilities to sales	12.0%	16.1%
Pressing to patient current liabilities—one item.		
Liabilities (short-term loans payable plus		
commercial paper/accounts payable)	3.0	5.4

REPAIR

- Negotiate extension of the maturity dates on loans.
- Negotiate lower interest rates on loans.
- Defer the payment of loans for one year.
- Offer creditors the opportunity to convert their debt into stock of the corporation at a favorable rate.
- Issue common and preferred stock at a favorable price to provide equity funds in order to improve the mix in the capital structure by lowering the debt to equity ratio.
- Sell assets to meet debt payments.
- Assign accounts receivable.

PREVENTION TECHNIQUES

- Set a maximum debt ceiling for the company that cannot be exceeded in any case.
- Institute a policy of buying assets only when operations absolutely require them.
- Negotiate open lines of credit to assure that funds will be available as needed.
- Review loan provisions, such as acceleration clauses stipulating that the loan is immediately due if an installment payment is

missed or the debt/equity ratio increases above a specified percentage. Compare existing terms of debt with the company's actual financial status to ascertain the degree to which the current position exceeds the compliance requirement.

- Use spontaneous sources of financing because they result from typical operating activities. They are essentially interest-free funds and should be extended to their maximum.
- If the company is a seasonal business that is a net borrower, try to use more long-term financing.
- Arrange to have debt mature during the company's profitable season rather than a period of slow sales.
- Do not incur debt when the return earned on borrowed funds is less than the after-tax cost of that debt.
- Issue lower-cost debt, such as commercial paper.
- Avoid making unrealistic promises about future earnings and profits. If the financial projection is conservative, a bank or financing institution is more likely to believe it and extend credit on favorable terms.
- Issue stock rather than cash dividends, so that cash is available to pay down debt.
- Establish a sinking fund and make payments into it each period so that funds are available to retire debt at maturity.

SPILLOVER EFFECTS

If debt is excessive, the interest on further financing will be higher because of the greater risk. Additional financing may even be totally unavailable. If the business cannot meet its debt payments, it may be forced into bankruptcy.

Excessive interest and principal payment obligations may also make it necessary to alter the dividend policy by omitting one or more dividend payments. This will have a negative impact on the market price of outstanding shares and later public offerings.

See also in this chapter: Inadequate Liquidity *and* INSOLVENCY.

PROBLEM
OFF-BALANCE-SHEET LIABILITIES

SYMPTOM

Prospective liabilities are not reported on the balance sheet.

CAUSE

The company has obligated itself for some time in the future. For example, guarantees of future performance and postretirement benefits may involve considerable deferred expenditures.

ANALYSIS

Off-balance-sheet financing is an attempt to generate monies by borrowing without having to record the liability on the financial statements. The dollar amount of an off-balance-sheet liability must be determined and recognized as a future drain on corporate financial resources.

Example: In Company N's pension plan, the projected benefit obligation is $6 million, while the accumulated benefit obligation is $5 million. The projected benefit obligation is the discounted value of future pension benefit payments to retired employees based on future salaries, while the accumulated benefit obligation is the discounted value of future pension benefit payments to retired employees based on current salaries. In this case, the company has an off-balance-sheet obligation of $1 million, the difference.

REPAIR

Off-balance-sheet liabilities may be funded through insurance, such as insurance against product liability.

PREVENTION TECHNIQUES

- Incorporate options and other protective provisions into lease agreements.
- Avoid agreements for future transactions.
- Minimize employee benefits.

SPILLOVER EFFECTS

The future payment of an off-balance sheet liability will reduce a company's cash position and liquidity. If the amount is substantial, such as huge damages in a lawsuit that are not covered by insurance, insolvency and bankruptcy are possible.

PROBLEM
DEFICIENT ASSET USE AND TURNOVER
SYMPTOMS

* Declining sales and profits.
* Idle capacity.
* Breakdowns.
* Low output relative to input.
* Buildup in inventory or receivables.
* Inactive use of assets.

CAUSES

* Inefficient or obsolete equipment.
* Multishift operations.
* Temporary changes in demand.
* Interruptions in the supply of raw materials and parts.
* Poor production scheduling.
* Inadequate supervision.

ANALYSIS

Asset utilization has as its ultimate measure the amount of sales generated, because sales are the first and essential step to profits. No assets should be held unless they contribute to revenue or generate income.

Asset utilization and turnover ratios that are useful here include:

* *Accounts receivable turnover See also in this chapter*: INADEQUATE LIQUIDITY.
* *Inventory turnover. See* INADEQUATE LIQUIDITY.
* *Sales to cash.* A high ratio may indicate a cash shortage. A low one may reflect the holding of idle and unnecessary cash balances.
* *Sales to working capital.* A high ratio may indicate inadequate working capital, which reflects negatively on liquidity.
* *Sales to fixed assets.* A low ratio means fixed assets are being used inefficiently or are obsolete, because they are not generating suffi-

cient sales. There may also be excess capacity and interruptions in the supply of raw materials.

- *Sales to total assets.* A low ratio indicates that the assets of the business are not generating adequate revenue. A low ratio of sales to machinery floor space machinery would similarly indicate inefficient utilization of space.

REPAIR

- Improve asset turnover by increasing sales, reducing investment, or both.
- Use assets more efficiently.
- Sell off unused or inactive assets so that the cash obtained can be used elsewhere (such as to pay debt).
- Be sure fixed assets are functioning properly. Repairs and maintenance may be necessary to improve efficiency.
- Lease equipment if production of a new product line has an uncertain period of benefit.
- Accelerate collections.
- Computerize inventory records and order systems.

PREVENTION TECHNIQUES

- Institute a regular program of overhaul or modernization.
- Compare the investment in assets to the value of the output produced. If assets are excessive, consolidate present operations, perhaps by selling some of the assets and investing the proceeds for a higher return, or by using them to expand into a more profitable area.

SPILLOVER EFFECTS

A cash shortage may result in a liquidity crisis if the business has no other available sources of funds. Inadequate utilization of capital facilities will mean lower sales and earnings. Inactive assets result in excessive costs.

See also in this chapter: INADEQUATE LIQUIDITY, LOW RATE OF RETURN, *and* POOR PROFITABILITY AND GROWTH.

PROBLEM
LOW RATE OF RETURN

SYMPTOMS

- High management turnover.
- Lower earnings estimates issued by brokerage analysts.
- Lower stock rankings published in financial newspapers and business weeklies.
- A drop in bond ratings.

CAUSES

- Declining sales.
- Inability to raise prices.
- Lower profit margins because of excessive costs.
- Lower asset turnover.

ANALYSIS

Return on investment (ROI), which relates net income to invested capital (total assets), is a standard for evaluating how efficiently management employs the average dollar invested in a firm's assets, whether that dollar came from owners or creditors. A better ROI can also translate directly into a higher return on stockholder equity.

In the past, financial managers have tended to look only at the margin earned, ignoring the turnover of assets. Yet excessive funds tied up in assets can be as much a burden on profitability as excessive expenses. The Du Pont Corporation was the first major company to recognize the importance of looking at both net profit margin and total asset turnover in assessing its performance. The ROI breakdown, known as the Du Pont formula, is expressed as a product of these two factors:

$$\text{ROI} = \frac{\text{Net profit after taxes}}{\text{Total assets}} = \frac{\text{Net profit after taxes}}{\text{Sales}} = \frac{\text{Sales}}{\text{Total assets}}$$

$$= \text{net profit margin x total asset turnover.}$$

The Du Pont formula combines the income statement and balance sheet for this otherwise static measure of performance. Net profit margin measures profitability or operating efficiency.. It is the percentage of profit earned on sales, which shows how many cents attach to each dollar of sales. On the other hand, total asset turnover measures how well a company manages its assets. It is the number of times by which the investment in assets turns over each year to generate sales.

The breakdown of ROI is based on the thesis that the profitability of a firm is directly related to its ability to manage assets efficiently and to control expenses effectively.

Generally, a better management performance as shown in a high or above average ROI produces a higher return to equity holders. However, even a poorly managed company that suffers from below-average performance can generate an above-average return on stockholder equity, simply called the return on equity (ROE). This is because borrowed funds can magnify the returns a company's profits represent to its stockholders.

Another version of the Du Pont formula, called the modified Du Pont formula, reflects this effect. The formula ties together ROI and the degree of financial leverage (use of borrowed funds). Financial leverage is measured by the equity multiplier, which is the ratio of a company's total asset base to its equity investment (stated another way, the ratio of dollars of assets held to dollars of stockholder equity). It is calculated by dividing total assets by stockholder equity. This measurement indicates how much of a company's assets are financed by stockholder equity and how much by borrowed funds:

$$\text{ROE} = \frac{\text{Net profit after taxes}}{\text{Stockholder's equity}} = \frac{\text{Net profit after taxes}}{\text{Total assets}} \times \frac{\text{Total assets}}{\text{Stockholders' equity}}$$

ROE measures the returns earned on the investment of both preferred and common stockholders. Use of the equity multiplier to convert ROI to ROE reflects the impact of the leverage (use of debt) on stockholders' returns.

$$\text{Equity multiplier} = \frac{\text{Total assets}}{\text{Stockholders' equity}} \times \frac{1}{(1\text{-Debt ratio})}$$

Example: Assume stockholder equity of $45,000 and total assets of $100,000. Then,

$$\text{Equity multiplier} = \frac{\text{Total assets}}{\text{Stockholders' equity}} \quad \frac{\$100,000}{\$45,000} = 2.22$$

$$= \frac{1}{(1\text{-Debt ratio})} = \frac{1}{1\text{-}0.55} \quad \frac{1}{0.45} = 2.22$$

$$ROE = \frac{\text{Net profit after taxes}}{\text{Stockholder's equity}} = \frac{\$18,000}{\$45,000} = 40\%$$

$$= ROI \times \text{Equity multiplier} = 18\% \times 2.22 = 40\%.$$

If the company used only equity, the 18 percent ROI would equal ROE. However, 55 percent of its capital is supplied by creditors ($45,000/$100,000 = 45 percent is the equity-to-asset ratio; $55,000/$100,000 = 55 percent is the debt ratio). Since the 18 percent ROI goes entirely to stockholders who put up only 45 percent of the capital, the ROE is higher than 18 percent. This example indicates that the company is using leverage (debt) favorably.

If the assets in which the funds are invested can earn more than the fixed rate of return required by creditors, the leverage is positive and common stockholders benefit. This formula enables the company to break its ROE into a profit margin portion (net profit margin), an efficiency-of-asset-utilization portion (total asset turnover), and a use-of-leverage portion (equity multiplier). It shows that the company can raise shareholder return by employing leverage, taking on more debt, to help finance growth.

Since financial leverage affects net profit margin through added interest costs, financial managers must look at each piece of the ROE equation within the context of the whole in order to maximize the return for stockholders. They must determine what combination of asset return and leverage will work best in the company's competitive environment. The relative contributions of the net profit margin and asset turnover ratio in the ROI relationship differ from industry to industry.

REPAIR

To enhance ROI:
- Improve margin by reducing expenses, raising selling prices, or increasing sales faster than expenses.
- Improve turnover by increasing sales while holding investment in assets relatively constant, or by reducing assets.
- Improve both.

PREVENTION TECHNIQUES

No ROI is satisfactory for all companies. A company's structure and size influence the rate considerably. A company with a diversified product line might have only a fair return rate when all products are pooled in the analysis. In such cases, it is advisable to establish separate objectives for each line as well as for the total company.

Successful operations must work to optimize the combination of profits, sales, and capital employed, which will vary depending on the nature of the business and its products. An industry with products tailored to customer specifications will have different margins and turnover ratios than industries that mass-produce highly competitive consumer goods.

SPILLOVER EFFECTS

- Layoffs.
- Downsizing.
- Declining profitability.
- Lower market price of stock and bonds.
- Increased cost of financing.
- Lack of financing.
- Corporate insolvency and bankruptcy.

See also in this chapter: LACK OF RESIDUAL INCOME. *In Chapter 2:* POOR CREDIT RATING. *In Chapter 4:* UNPROFITABLE PROFIT CENTERS. *In Chapter 7:* DROP IN BOND RATING *and* MARKET PRICE OF STOCK FAILING.

PROBLEM
LACK OF RESIDUAL INCOME
SYMPTOMS

While a business shows net income, it is only minimally profitable or is in fact actually losing money. This can also be true of individual divisions. They may report a profit but not be doing as well as it seems.

CAUSES

• Poor profitability.
• High opportunity cost on total assets employed.

ANALYSIS

For a company, the higher the ratio of residual income to net income, the better.

Residual income equals net income less minimum return (cost of capital) times total assets. Residual income that is less than reported earnings indicates a financial problem.

Example: Company G's net income is $632,800, total assets are $4,600,000, and its cost of capital is 13.4 percent. Residual income is arrived at as follows:

Net income	= $632,800
Less minimum return x total assets 13.40% x $4,600,000	= 616,400
Residual income	= $16,400

The ratio of residual to net income is 2.6 percent ($16,400/$632,800). This percentage is low, indicating that the company is not earning enough economic income, taking into account the opportunity cost of tying up money in the business.

An increasing trend in residual to net income may indicate stronger profitability because the business is earning enough to cover its imputed cost of capital.

Residual income may be projected by division, center, or specific program to assure that the company's rate of return on alternative investments is met or improved upon by each segment of the business. By doing so, you are assured that segments are not employing corporate credit for less return than could be obtained by owning marketable securities or through investment in a different business segment.

Residual income for a division is calculated the same way as it is for a company, using the divisional figures. The minimum return is based on the company's total cost of financing adjusted for divisional risk.

Example: Divisional earnings are $150,000, average available assets are $2,000,000, and the cost of capital is 9 percent.

Residual income is arrived at as follows:

Divisional net income   = $150,000

Less minimum return x average available assets

(9% x $2,000,000)   =   180,000

Residual income   = ($30,000)

Although the division has earned $150,000, it has really lost $30,000, considering the opportunity cost of tying up the assets in the division.

The trend in residual income to total available assets should certainly be examined in appraising divisional performance. A target residual income may be formulated as an objective for the division manager. There are many benefits to using residual income analysis:

• The same asset may be required to earn the same return rate throughout the company, regardless of the division in which the asset is located.

• Different return rates may be employed for different types of assets, depending on riskiness.

• Different return rates may be assigned to different divisions, depending on the risk associated with those divisions.

REPAIR

• Increase profitability (e.g., through immediate cost-cutting).

• Use assets more efficiently..

PREVENTION TECHNIQUES

• Obtain lower-cost alternative financing.

• Improve the productivity of resources.

SPILLOVER EFFECTS

A low or negative residual income may threaten continued financial viability and success of a company because, after considering the imputed cost of financing, the company is really losing money.

See also in this chapter: LOW RATE OF RETURN. *In Chapter 4:* UNPROFITABLE PROFIT CENTERS.

PROBLEM
HIGH CASH-REALIZATION RISK
IN ASSETS

SYMPTOMS

- Management cannot convert assets into cash quickly because the assets are of questionable value.
- The assets have no separate realizable value and cannot be sold, or have low cash value and high risk.

CAUSE

Nonliquid assets no longer have their original value.

ANALYSIS

The more the dollar amounts of a company's assets are in the high-risk category, the more assets and earnings are overstated—earnings are overstated because the assets should have been written down to recognize the decline in their value. For analytical purposes, useful ratios are the percentage of high-risk assets to total assets and to sales.

Example: Company C reports receivables of $4,000,000, which include the following high-risk receivables:

Notes receivable arising from extensions of unpaid balances from delinquent customers	= $100,000
Advances to politically and economically unstable foreign governments	= <u>200,000</u>
High-risk receivables	= $300,000

Thus, of the receivables reported in the balance sheet, $300,000, or 7.5 percent, are of questionable quality.

Multipurpose assets are deemed to be of higher quality than single-purpose assets because they can be converted to cash more quickly. It is important to try to maintain market price stability in assets, because if their market prices fluctuate, it may be difficult to sell them.

It is also important to consider the impact of changing government policies on the company. There is an exposure to risk for companies because of increasing regulation and an increasing number of decisions by regulatory bodies.

REPAIR

- Sell low-quality assets as soon as possible, before their values diminish further.
- Correct inventory that fails to meet regulatory standards before its sale.
- Factor in accounts receivable and purchase insurance protection on questionable assets.

PREVENTION TECHNIQUES

- Avoid high cash-realization-risk assets.
- Minimize expenditures for assets like leasehold improvements.
- Do not acquire high-risk companies.
- Control work-in-process levels.
- Avoid costly startup operations.
- Refrain from moving production facilities.
- Improve credit policies.
- Reevaluate credit policies for new customers.
- Minimize operations in politically and economically unstable geographic areas.
- Avoid making low-quality investments.
- Establish a committee to appraise the acquisition of major assets.

SPILLOVER EFFECTS

A change in asset quality will also effect a change in profits and cash flow. The sale, discard, or malfunction of one operational asset may adversely affect the profitability of related assets. If a company has many high-risk assets, when it faces a cash flow emergency it may be unable to sell them to meet debt obligations.

PROBLEM
POOR PROFITABILITY AND GROWTH

SYMPTOMS

- Declining earnings.
- A negative or minimal growth rate.
- Lack of funds to remain competitive or to expand.
- Erosion of sales base.

CAUSES

- Low return rates on assets and sales.
- Failure to control costs.
- Loss in market share.
- Inability to take advantage of technological advances.
- Low morale and high turnover.
- High degree of risk.
- Losses of uninsured assets.
- Inexperienced management.

Example: A decision to build a new plant or expand into a foreign market may influence the performance of the company over the entire next decade. When the decision is made to build the plant, management is usually uncertain about annual operating coats and inflows, product life, interest rates, economic conditions, and technological change. Thus, a wrong decision can adversely affect the company's long-term financial status.

ANALYSIS

The profitability and growth rate of the business should be compared over time and with the performance of competing companies and industry norms. The following ratios should also be analyzed:

$$\text{Growth rate in retained earnings} = \frac{\text{Net income - Dividends}}{\text{Common stockholders' equity}}$$

A lower ratio suggests that a company is unable to generate funds internally and must rely on external sources, such as debt and equity.

$$\frac{\text{Growth rate in earnings}}{\text{per share EPS}} = \frac{\text{EPS (End of period) - EPS (Beginning of period)}}{\text{EPS (Beginning of period)}}$$

$$\text{Profit margin} = \frac{\text{Net income}}{\text{Sales}}$$

A low profit margin means that the earnings generated from revenue are deficient, reflecting poor earning power. The profit margin provides clues to pricing, cost structure, and production efficiency.

$$\text{Gross profit margin} = \frac{\text{Gross profit}}{\text{Sales}}$$

A lower gross profit margin indicates that the business cannot control its production costs.

$$\text{Return on Investments} = \frac{\text{Net income}}{\text{Total assets}}$$

A low ROI means that the earnings generated by the use of assets in the business is deficient.

Growth rate may be expressed in terms of a compounded annual rate:

Compounded annual rate of growth = Fn = P x T1(i, n).

where   Fn = Future value amount.

P = Present value amount.

T1(i, n) = future value factor based on interest rate (i) and number of periods (n).

Solving this for T1, we get:

$$T1(i,n) = \frac{Fn}{P}$$

Example: Assume a company has earnings per share of $2.50 in 20XX, and 10 years later EPS has increased to $3.70. The compound annual rate of growth in earnings per share is computed as follows:

F10 = $3.70 and P = $2.50.

Therefore,

$$T1\,(i,\,10) = \frac{\$3.70}{\$2.50} = 1.48$$

From the future value of $1 table (Table 5.3), a T1 of 1.48 at 10 years is at i = 4%. The compound annual rate of growth is therefore 4 percent.

TABLE 5.3. FUTURE VALUE OF $1 = T1(i, N)

Periods	4%	6%	8%	10%	12%	14%	20%
1	1.040	1.060	1.080	1.100	1.120	1.140	1.200
2	1.082	1.124	1.166	1.210	1.254	1.300	1.440
3	1.125	1.191	1.260	1.331	1.405	1.482	1.728
4	1.170	1.263	1.361	1.464	1.574	1.689	2.074
5	1.217	1.338	1.469	1.611	1.762	1.925	2.488
6	1.265	1.419	1.587	1.772	1.974	2.195	2.986
7	1.316	1.504	1.714	1.949	2.211	2.502	3.583
8	1.369	1.594	1.851	2.144	2.476	2.853	4.300
9	1.423	1.690	1.999	2.359	2.773	3.252	5.160
10	1.480	1.791	2.159	2.594	3.106	3.707	6.192
11	1.540	1.898	2.332	2.853	3.479	4.226	7.430
12	1.601	2.012	2.518	3.139	3.896	4.818	8.916
13	1.665	2.133	2.720	3.452	4.364	5.492	10.699
14	1.732	2.261	2.937	3.798	4.887	6.261	12.839
15	1.801	2.397	3.172	4.177	5.474	7.138	15.407
16	1.873	2.540	3.426	4.595	6.130	8.137	18.488
17	1.948	2.693	3.700	5.055	6.866	9.277	22.186
18	2.026	2.854	3.996	5.560	7.690	10.575	26.623
19	2.107	3.026	4.316	6.116	8.613	12.056	31.948
20	2.191	3.207	4.661	5.728	9.646	13.743	38.338
30	3.243	5.744	10.063	17.450	29.960	50.950	237.380
40	4.801	10.286	21.725	45.260	93.051	188.880	1469.800

REPAIR

- Introduce new product lines.
- Enter into joint ventures or merge with innovative companies.
- Diversify.
- Sell off unprofitable branches and subsidiaries.
- Replace obsolete assets.
- Obtain adequate insurance coverage for all assets.
- Increase the selling prices of products.
- Increase sales volume.
- Cut costs.
- Renegotiate union contracts and employee benefits.
- Improve manufacturing efficiency.
- Enhance return rates on assets and sales.
- Reduce risk.

- Improve worker relations.
- Redirect the sales effort to improve profit margin.
- Increase asset turnover and cash collection policies.

Selling, general, and administrative expenses are easier to control than cost of sales because they are internal and therefore subject to cost reduction programs.

PREVENTION TECHNIQUES

- Draw up an advertising and sales promotion plan to increase sales and reduce costs.
- Implement a cost-reduction program.
- Identify and correct problem areas.
- Use computerized reports and analyses.
- Institute cash and inventory management programs.

SPILLOVER EFFECTS

Lack of earnings and negative growth may ultimately lead to a poor cash position that creates operating, liquidity, and solvency problems. Poor earnings and growth will result in a lower market price for company stock and bonds, a deteriorating credit rating, increased cost of financing, and a lack of funds to support operations. If corporate earning power is at a minimum or nonexistent, the business may fail because it is not generating sufficient cash earnings. The company may also be targeted for takeover.

See also in this chapter: DEFICIENT ASSET USE AND TURNOVER, LOW RATE OF RETURN, *and* POOR-QUALITY EARNINGS.

PROBLEM
POOR-QUALITY EARNINGS

SYMPTOMS

- Lower P/E ratio.
- Higher cost of financing.
- Unavailability of suitable financing.
- Higher compensating balances and security required for loan agreements.
- Deterioration in the company's bond rating.

CAUSES

- Unrealistic accounting policies and estimates.
- Inadequate provision for enhancement of present and future earning power (e.g., repairs and maintenance).
- Instability in operations and earnings.
- Unjustified reduction in discretionary costs, depriving the business of investments needed for future growth (e.g., advertising, research and development).
- Decline in profitability.
- Subjective and uncertain accounting estimates associated with recognition of revenue and expenses (the further revenue and expense recognition is from the point of cash receipt and cash payment, the less objective the transaction and the more subjective the interpretations).
- High cash-realization risk of assets.
- High fixed cost structure.
- Susceptibility to the business cycle.
- Business risk.
- Low ratio of cash earnings to net income.
- Low ratio of residual income to net income.
- High ratio of sales returns and allowances to sales.
- Deficient return on assets.
- Lack of diversification.

ANALYSIS

Poor-quality earnings are earnings that do not relate reasonably to the business operations of a company within a given period of time (e.g., the most realistic accounting alternative was not employed). When two competitive companies use alternative accounting policies, financial analysts adjust the two net incomes to a common basis to reduce the diversity in accounting. Information provided in footnotes may help in the restatement process. For instance, there may be disclosure of what the earnings effect would have been if another method of accounting (e.g., the inventory method) had been used.

A weak functional relationship between sales and net income may indicate that a company is manipulating its earnings.

Example: A company's ratio of net income to sales was as follows for the period 20XI to 20X4:

20X1	20X2	20X3	20X4
12%	3%	20%	(5%)

Because the pattern indicates a weak association between net income and sales, some manipulation may be inferred.

Analysts can estimate true earnings per share by making quantitative adjustments to reported EPS, with the revised figure reflecting more realistically the earning power of a company. The conversion process will result in a higher quality-of-earnings figure. Analysts often adjust reported EPS for low-quality items.

Example: A company's reported EPS of $10 includes numerous low-quality components. These items are shown in Table 5.4 as deductions from reported EPS. Note that the items shown were chosen with a view to making the adjustment process clearer. In reality, of course, reported EPS would be adjusted upward or downward for a variety of other reconciling items. An example of an upward adjustment would be adding back in the effect of an unjustified accounting cushion arising from overestimated provisions for warranty service or for bad debt.

REPAIR

• Incur expenditures needed for future successful operations.
• Make realistic expense and liability provisions.
• Provide for realistic recognition of revenue.
• Avoid cutting costs necessary for successful operations.
• Write-down overvalued assets.

PREVENTION TECHNIQUES

• Use realistic accounting methods and assumptions.
• Avoid manipulative accounting practices.
• Avoid deferring expenditures for questionable future benefits.
• Diversify operations.
• Enter countercyclical lines of business.
• Reduce risk exposure.
• Combat the adverse effects of inflation.
• Adjust the cost structure toward variable rather than fixed costs.

TABLE 5.4. ADJUSTMENT OF EPS FOR EARNINGS QUALITY

Reported EPS *$10.00*

Deductions in order lo arrive at an EPS of "acceptable quality:"

Unjustified cutbacks in discretionary costs (e.g., advertising) as a percent of sales . . 0.02

Decline in the ratio of bad debts to sales that is not warranted by experience 0.03

One-time gains (gain on the sale of land) that are not expected to recur.......... 0.04

Income derived from the sale of acquired assets that were recorded at suppressed
amounts at the time of a pooling transaction 0.05

Inventory profits.. 0.06

Accounting changes designed to bolster earnings (LIFO to FIFO).............. 0.07

Lower pension expense arising from an unrealistic change in
pension assumptions (increase in the actuarially assumed interest rate).......... 0.08

Increase in deferred expenditures that do not have future economic benefit....... 0.09

Items included in inventory that were previously expensed
(labor, interest, administrative coats), assuming such items have no future utility . . . 0.02

Items included in plant and equipment that were previously expensed
(e.g., maintenance costs)... 0.03

Lower provision (relative to prior years) for cost overruns on long-term
construction contracts 0.04

Increase in expenses (relative to prior years) charged to reserve accounts 0.05

Unjustified reduction in reserve accounts 0.06

Incremental capitalized interest relative to prior year 0.07

Underaccrual of expenses (or reserve provision).......................... 0.08

One-time earnings increment arising from a change in revenue recognition policy . . 0.09

Lower effective tax rate arising from a one-time tax benefit, such as a
foreign tax credit... 0.02

"Acceptable Quality" EPS *$9.10*

SPILLOVER EFFECTS

Poor earnings quality:

- Increases the cost of borrowing.
- Increases debt relative to equity financing, because investors are less inclined to buy the company's stock because of its perceived lower quality.
- May lead to business failure because of the risk assigned to the company on account of its dubious earnings quality.
- Decreases the market price of company stock and bonds.
- Lowers the company's credit rating.
- May increase employee turnover because of the higher probability of business failure.
- Increases the collateral requirements for loans.

PROBLEM
UNSTABLE OPERATIONS AND EARNINGS

SYMPTOMS

Fluctuating sales, costs, and profitability over time.

CAUSES

Whenever operations are subject to risk from industrial, corporate, political, or economic factors, there will be uncertainty. If there is high turnover among managers, operating policy will be inconsistent.

If the outside auditors are changed, the financial reporting system may be affected because of differences audit approaches and philosophies. If accounting changes are made in methods and estimates, accounting policies will be inconsistent.

Variability in operations may also exist because:

• Management is taking excessive risks.

• High financial leverage prevents the firm from meeting principal and interest on debt when earnings decline. (A high degree of operating leverage means a structure that contains significant fixed costs. As volume decreases, fixed costs cannot be cut in the short run. The result is a dramatic fallow in profits.)

• The company is overly susceptible to the business cycle or to seasonality.

• Unreliable sources and cost of raw materials for production cause instability in manufacturing operations and the resultant earnings fluctuations.

• Product sales are only to a few large industrial users, which is risky.

• The political environment is unstable.

ANALYSIS

We rely on the likelihood of repetitiveness in projecting future earnings. Therefore, we need to separate stable elements of income and expense from those that are random and erratic. Earnings that derive from recurring transactions related to the basic business of the company are of *higher quality* than those resulting from isolated transactions.

Determine the extent to which earnings reflect one-time gains and losses that are not part of the basic business of the firm and that will thus distort the current year's income as a predictor of future earnings. For example, a one-time gain will result in higher than normal earnings for the year. Such items should be eliminated from net income in determining relevant earnings. To determine the extent to which net income is being distorted, it is necessary to compute the percent of one-time gains and losses to net income and to sales.

Example: The figures shown in Table 5.5 are extracted from company C's comparative income statements.

The rising percentage of net one-time gains to sales and to net income indicates that earnings quality is deteriorating.

TABLE 5.5. EARNINGS ADJUSTMENT TO NET OUT ONE-TIME GAINS AND LOSSES

	20X0	*20X1*	*20X2*
Sales	$100,000	$105,000	$113,000
Net Income	20,000	22,000	27,000
Net one-time gains (one-time gains lessone-time losses)	5,000	7,000	10,000
Ratios:			
Net one-time gains to sales	5.0%	6.7%	8.8%
Net one-time gains to net income	25.0%	31.8%	37.0%

Determine the trends in operating income sources (sales) and nonoperating income sources (lease and royalty income) over the last five years. Nonoperating income may be more stable, and therefore of higher quality, than operating income. Evaluate nonoperating income to determine the extent to which it is recurring and acts to stabilize total income.

Look at the current environment to see if there are likely to be any changes in demand for the company's products or services. If you conclude that greater dependability is likely in one or more nonoperating income sources, look at the trend in the percentage of such nonoperating items to sales and to net income. Rising trends reflect higher earnings quality. In evaluating the riskiness of a business, examine the stability of the earnings trend. The trend in income is considerably more significant than its absolute size.

Earnings stability can be measured in terms of average reported earnings, average pessimistic earnings, standard deviation, coefficient of variation, instability index, and beta. These techniques should be applied to earnings over a long period, from five to ten years. The greater the variation in earnings indicated by the following six measures, the worse for the business.

1. *Average reported earnings.* Averaging earnings over, say, five years will smooth out abnormal and erratic income statement components as well as cyclical effects. Thus, the average is a better measure of earning power than net income for a particular year.

2. *Average pessimistic earnings.* This is average earnings based on the worst possible business activity. This figure is useful only where the business is quite risky and you wish to provide for such risk. The first step is to restate reported earnings to minimum earnings for each year, and then find the average.

3. *Standard deviation* is calculated as follows:

$$SD = \sqrt{\frac{\sum(y-\bar{y})^2}{n}}$$

where y = Reported earnings for period t.
y = Average earnings.
n = Number of years.

A high standard deviation indicates greater risk, because it measures the variability of earnings against expected earnings. It is an absolute measure of instability.

4. *Coefficient of variation* is calculated as follows:

$$SV = \frac{SD}{\bar{y}}$$

The coefficient of variation, which represents the degree of risk per unit of return, is used to appraise relative instability in earnings. The higher the coefficient of variation in the earnings of a business, the higher the risk in its earnings stream.

5. *Instability index of earnings* is calculated as follows:

$$I = \sqrt{\frac{\sum (y-y^t)^2}{n}}$$

where y^t = trend earnings for period *t*, and is calculated by:
$$y^t = a + bt.$$
where a = Dollar intercept.
  b = Slope of trend line.
  t = Time period.
A simple equation solved by computer is used to determine trend income. The index reflects the deviation between actual income and trend income. The higher the index, the lower the quality of earnings.

6. *Beta* is determined via a computer run for the following equation:

$$r_j = a + B_j r_m.$$
where r_j = return on security j.
  a = constant.
  B_j = beta for security j.
  r_m = return on a market index such as the S&P 500 index.

Beta is a measure of the undiversifiable risk of a stock. It helps analyze the risk-return trade-off. A high beta means that the company's stock price has shown more fluctuation than change in the market index, indicating that it is a risky security. High variability in stock price may indicate greater business risk, instability in the firm's past earnings trend, or lower earnings quality. For example, a beta of 1.6 means that the firm's stock price rises or falls 60 percent more than the market. Over time, a stock may have a positive beta in some years and a negative beta in others.

REPAIR

- Manage your raw materials needs downstream. Enter into a forward contract to take delivery of raw materials at a set price at a future date. Correct uncertainty of a raw material source by vertical integration or entering into a joint venture. Establish alternative sources of supply for raw materials. Constantly review raw materials prices and future availability in trade and financial publications.

- Enter into foreign currency futures contracts to lock in a fixed rate.
- Reduce instability in earnings due to a high fixed cost structure by moving toward a variable cost structure, increasing the ratio of variable costs to fixed costs.
- Protect a reliable source of earnings, such as service contracts or replacement parts on products previously sold.
- Buy adequate liability insurance to guard against possible lawsuits.
- Develop or promote a product line of low-unit-cost items to provide income during a strong economy and cushion declining demand during recession.
- Add products that have different seasonal appeal and demand.

PREVENTION TECHNIQUES

- Undertake a risk-management program to find ways to curtail risk.
- Minimize uncertainty by entering countercyclical or noncyclical lines of business.
- Produce and sell products that are less affected by the business cycle.
- Emphasize stable products and better-grade investments.
- Diversify the customer base to protect against adverse changes in the economy or in one or two industries.

SPILLOVER EFFECTS

- When operations and profits are unstable, it is hard to predict future earnings and stock price.
- Variability in earnings and uncertainty in operations result in a lower market price of stock, lower issuance price for bond offerings, higher cost of financing to compensate for the increased risk, and lower credit rating.
- The uncertainties facing a business may be of such magnitude that net income has little predictive value.

See also in this chapter: POOR-QUALITY EARNINGS. *In Chapter 6:* EXCESSIVE OPERATING LEVERAGE. *In Chapter 8:* LACK OF DIVERSIFICATION. *In Chapter 11:* REVENUE BASE EROSION.

PROBLEM
UNSTABLE INCOME

SYMPTOMS

- The existence of an opportunist and temporary market (such as the early market for computers).
- Extra product demand, coupled with a sharp upward acceleration of prices.
- Sudden and unexpected developments that depress revenue.
- Variances in selling prices and costs.

CAUSES

- The product mix is positively *correlated*, meaning that demands for products moves upward or downward together. (Examples of such products are automobiles, tires, and steel.)
- The company is unable to introduce new products.
- The product line consists primarily of items that are declining in demand or are in the initial stages of research and development.
- A product is nearing the end of its life cycle.
- The customer base consists only of a few large concerns.
- The company's main income comes from a single significant contract (e.g., with the government) or a single product.
- Temporary income is a high percentage of total revenue.
- The company's products are susceptible to changes in the business cycle and to seasonality.
- The product line lacks diversification.
- The market for the product line is subject to rapid changes in demand and taste.
- Export sales to a major foreign market suddenly disappear when that country develops its own domestic production.

ANALYSIS

Determine the extent to which earnings reflect unstable sources of income that are not part of the basic business of the firm. Operating income (sales) should be of higher quality than nonoperating income (e.g., interest revenue) because it represents earnings generated from selling the company's products. However, if nonoperating income is more stable than sales, it is of higher quality than operating income. Evaluate nonoperating income to determine the extent to which it is recurring and acts to stabilize total income.

Stability in product revenue can be determined by computing the standard deviation in sales over five to 10 years (see the previous section). A high standard deviation indicates instability in income. A coefficient of variation may also be computed to appraise relative instability with other competing companies.

Example: Company L has the following income history:

20X0	$100,000
20X1	110,000
20X2	80,000
20X3	120,000
20X4	140,000

The standard deviation in sales is:

$$\text{Standard deviation} = \sqrt{\frac{\sum (y-y^t)^2}{n}}$$

$$\bar{y} = \sum \frac{y}{n} = \frac{100,000 + 110,000 + 80,000 + 120,000 + 140,000}{5} = \frac{550,000}{5} = 110,000$$

Year	$(y-\bar{y})$	$(y-\bar{y})^2$
20X0	-10,000	100,000,000
20X1	0	0
20X2	-30,000	900,000,000
20X3	+10,000	100,000,000
20X4	+30,000	900,000,000
Total		2,000,000,000

$$\text{Standard deviation} = \sqrt{\frac{2,000,000,000}{5}} = \sqrt{400,000,000} = 20,000$$

The coefficient of variation in sales is:

$$\text{Coefficient of variation} = \frac{\text{Standard deviation}}{\bar{y}} = \frac{20,000}{110,000} = 18.2\%.$$

The more a product line is susceptible to variances in volume, price, and cost, the greater the revenue instability. Chart the variability in quantity, selling price, and cost of each major product line over one or more periods of time.

Evaluate how much revenue is derived from growth, mature, declining, and developmental products.

REPAIR

- Attempt to derive further revenues after each initial sales contact.
- Support first-time sales with maintenance contracts, follow-up sales (like those for batteries and flashcubes in the case of cameras), and replacement parts.
- Diversify the product line with *negatively correlated* (noncorrelated) items to provide income stability. With negative correlation, revenue obtained from one product increases while revenue from other products decreases. (Examples: Air conditioners and heaters.)
- Expand the product line to add complementary products. (For a firm selling air conditioners and heaters, complementary products could include insulating materials, thermostats, and home improvement materials.)

PREVENTIVE TECHNIQUES

- Emphasize products that are less affected by the business cycle.
- Attempt to change lines to more stable products.
- Develop a piggyback product base (similar products associated with the basic business).
- Sell low-priced products as well as more expensive goods as a built-in hedge in inflationary and recessionary periods.

- Move toward producing necessities that perform well in both good and bad economic times.
- Avoid novelty and nonessential goods.
- Sell to diversified industries to protect against cyclical turns in the economy.
- Reduce exposure to the effects of the economic cycle by entering noncyclical or countercyclical lines of business.
- Diversify geographically to reduce susceptibility to regional economic downturns.

SPILLOVER EFFECTS

Revenue instability leads to vacillating and erratic earnings that will negatively affect the market price of a company's debt and equity securities. The uncertainty of its income stream will make the company's future more uncertain.

See Chapter 4: WEAK SALES MIX.

PROBLEM
LOW PRICE/EARNINGS RATIO

SYMPTOM

Low market price of company stock.

CAUSES

- Investors lack confidence in the company's financial stability or growth potential. This may be due to the company's financial position, its trend in earnings, or the investing public's perception of the quality of its earnings.
- The market price of the stock has not increased proportionally with its EPS.
- Investors believe that the company will be less profitable in the future than its current earnings would seem to indicate.

ANALYSIS

The P/E ratio should be compared to the P/E ratios of competing companies in the same industry, with those of other companies, and with the market average. P/E ratios may be found in financial service publications or can be computed with the following equation:

$$\text{Price/earnings ratio} = \frac{\text{Market price per share}}{\text{Earnings per share}}$$

Example: The market prices per share of stock are $20 for 20X8 and $24 for 20X9. The EPS for 20X8 is $2 and for 20X9 $3. The P/E ratios are computed as:

$$\text{P/E ratio} = \frac{\text{Market price per share}}{\text{Earnings per share}} = \frac{\overset{20X8}{\$20}}{\$2} = \frac{\overset{20X9}{\$24}}{\$3} = 8$$

REPAIR

Convince investors that the company's low P/E multiple means that its stock is undervalued and is a bargain.

PREVENTION TECHNIQUES

- Improve the company's financial condition, including balance sheet posture and earnings.
- Reduce risk.
- Enhance operational stability.
- Expand, diversify, or sell off unprofitable branches and divisions.
- Hire better managers.
- Create a promotional campaign to emphasize company history, the quality of its products, and its potential for economic growth.

SPILLOVER EFFECTS

A low P/E ratio is considered to mean that the company may be a poor investment. Investors are likely to stay away, further depressing the market price of the stock. Failure to attract equity investors may cause creditors to demand increased interest rates. The higher cost of financing will reduce earnings.

Chapter 6
Costs Cutting
Into Profits

Excessive costs must be controlled. They will eat into profits and may turn them into losses. Cost control programs should be used to eliminate fat and inefficiency in the organization, taking care not to reduce costs needed for future viability of the business, such as those for repairs, research and development, and advertising.

Management may have a problem formulating financial decisions because cost information is inadequate or distorted. If raw materials are unavailable or available only at exorbitant rates, manufacturing problems will result. The company may be unable to grow by introducing new products or services for future growth because of high upfront costs. Incorrect pricing based on high or erroneous coat figures will lead to declining earnings.

The following problems are analyzed in this chapter:

• Excessive labor costs.
• Excessive operating leverage.
• Inadequate cost controls.
• Lack of cost information.
• Distorted cost information.
• Supplies more expensive or unavailable.
• Cost reductions hampering development.
• Reduced discretionary costs hurting the business.

- Upfront costs impeding project authorization.
- Pricing that lowers profits.

PROBLEM
EXCESSIVE LABOR COSTS

SYMPTOMS

- Inadequate funding for pension and health care benefits.
- A decline in earnings because wage and fringe benefit costs are not controlled.
- Excessive workers compensation claims.
- High employee turnover.
- Theft and sabotage of company assets.

CAUSES

- Too many concessions to unions.
- Poor employee performance and productivity.
- Lack of strong supervision.
- Inadequate employee training.
- Obsolete machinery and equipment.
- Inefficient production scheduling.
- Alcohol and drug abuse.
- Hiring the wrong employees or hiring more than necessary.
- Absenteeism.

ANALYSIS

- Compute trends in the ratios of labor costs to total costs, labor costs to sales, and labor costs to net income.
- Examine postretirement payouts.
- Compare company employee benefits with those provided by other companies in the industry.
- Compute the rate and efficiency variances for direct and indirect labor costs (*see Chapter 9*: ACTUAL COSTS EXCEEDING STANDARD COSTS).

REPAIR

- Negotiate with unions for give-backs in wages, fringe benefits, hours, and other working conditions.

- Pay the minimum wage possible for a particular position, give minimal wage increases, or if possible freeze salaries.
- Lay off employees to cut payroll.
- Institute a furlough (delay) in pay, or reduce working hours and workdays.
- Improve supervision by managers.
- Make sure more employees are not assigned to a specific task than are needed.
- Use temporary and per-diem personnel.
- Monitor employee time and charge it to specific jobs and customers.
- Control health care costs:
- Increase deductibles and reduce reimbursement payments to lower premium rates.
- Place caps on certain benefits.
- Require employees to contribute to their health plan.
- Switch to cheaper carriers.
- Institute low-cost health care centers (e.g., HIP, HMO).
- Require second opinions before authorizing operations.
- Remove some coverages from the health care package.
- Eliminate retiree health care benefits.
- Terminate coverage for employee beneficiaries.
- Encourage preventive health care.
- Institute a stock-based compensation plan.
- Give inefficient workers the option of transferring to a new facility or position.
- Help terminated employees find new employment.
- Operate with a small central staff.
- Increase selling prices for goods and services.

PREVENTION TECHNIQUES

- Hire a competent union negotiator or labor lawyer and support binding arbitration.
- Tie increases in wages to improvements in productivity.
- Design and implement actions to resolve employee problems like low productivity or poor workmanship.
- Improve production scheduling.
- Reassign workers to improve efficiency..

- Find out the reasons for absenteeism and low productivity.
- Offer early retirement incentives.
- Use a newsletter to communicate to employees the company's financial problems, how employees can help, and the possible adverse effects on employees if conditions do not improve.
- Conduct periodic meetings to further communicate with employees.
- Keep equipment in proper working order.
- Introduce continuous safety checks.
- Write detailed proper job descriptions.
- Evaluate the personnel department to make sure it is hiring the right people.
- Integrate the personnel staff into the planning process to enable them to evaluate job descriptions so that only the best-qualified employees are hired.
- Downsize the number of employees if future business is uncertain.
- Re-evaluate senior executive compensation, staffing, and performance.
- Reduce executive perks, including bonuses and expense accounts.
- Offer cash bonuses to employees who contribute workable ideas to save costs.

SPILLOVER EFFECTS

Failure to cap salaries and fringe benefits will drain cash and earnings and can lead to serious financial problems. Friction resulting from management-worker disputes may result in strikes and physical damage to property, plant, and equipment.

*

See also in this chapter: INADEQUATE COST CONTROLS. *In Chapter 10:* UNFUNDED RETIREMENT BENEFITS.

PROBLEM
EXCESSIVE OPERATING LEVERAGE

SYMPTOMS

- Significant earnings instability resulting from small changes in sales.
- A high breakeven point, indicating that more sales dollars are needed to cover total costs in order to earn zero profit.
- Difficulty adjusting costs to meet a changing revenue base.

CAUSE

Significant fixed costs are usually to blame. If sales decline, profitability will fall off sharply because fixed costs are constant. A business usually can only cut fixed costs over the long term.

ANALYSIS

Operating leverage can be measured using the following ratios:
- Fixed costs to total costs.
- Percentage change in operating income to percentage change in sales volume.
- Net income to fixed costs.

An increase in the first two or a decrease in the third may indicate higher fixed costs that may cause greater instability in operations and earnings.

When high operating leverage is combined with highly elastic product demand, earnings fluctuate sharply. Such conditions, though undesirable and leading to lower earnings quality, may be inherent in a company's operations (e.g., in the airline and auto industries).

The effects of operating leverage diminish as revenue increases above the breakeven point because the bases to which increases in earnings are compared are progressively larger. It may thus be advantageous to analyze the relationship between sales and the breakeven point when evaluating a company's earnings stability. A company with a high breakeven point is quite vulnerable to economic declines.

REPAIR

- To the extent possible, slash fixed costs.
- Expand sales to cover the costs that remain.

PREVENTION TECHNIQUE

Move toward a cost structure based on variable rather than fixed costs. The objective is thus to increase the percentage of variable to total costs. Variable costs can be adjusted more easily than fixed costs to meet changes in product demand.

SPILLOVER EFFECTS

Excessive operating leverage will sharply reduce profitability if sales decline, particularly in a recession. Failure to cut fixed costs in the long term may ultimately force a company into bankruptcy as its cash is drained to meet these static recurring charges.

See Chapter 4: PRODUCT OR SERVICE FAILING TO BREAK EVEN.

PROBLEM
INADEQUATE COST CONTROLS

SYMPTOMS

- Large variances in the cash disbursement reports between prices paid for identical quantities of the same raw materials.
- Labor variances showing up on job cost sheets due to:
- Differences in time spent performing identical tasks.
- Different hourly rates for employee overtime needed to solve unforeseen scheduling problems.
- Excessive raw materials required to manufacture a product.

CAUSES

- Lax or ineffective purchasing procedures.
- Lack of management control, resulting in inefficient operations and products of minimal or unacceptable quality.

ANALYSIS

- Instruct each department to set up standards for each product line.
- Plot the data corresponding to each standard. Visualizing the data creates an extended view of how the product is performing. Correlating standards to potential problems helps correct the situation before difficulties become crises.
- Measure the variance in, costs—the difference between actual costs and standard costs—inherent in the operations of the organization. (Standard costs are pre-established costs that are benchmarks against which actual costs of production can be measured). Use this analysis to determine the profitability and efficiency of operations. (*See in Chapter 9:* ACTUAL COSTS EXCEEDING BUDGETED COSTS *and* ACTUAL COSTS EXCEEDING STANDARD COSTS for the computation and analysis of variances.)

REPAIR

- Enforce a strict cost containment program. Hold each purchasing agent responsible for controlling material costs and each production supervisor responsible for maintaining standard labor costs.
- Arbitrate a price increase on a contracted project that is losing money.
- Reduce fluctuations of yields for raw materials purchased; decrease spending for raw materials by increasing their yields. This may be accomplished by frequent inspections during manufacturing. (Yield refers to the quantity of finished output produced from a predetermined or standard combination and amount of inputs, such as direct material or direct labor.)
- Tighten controls on spending, both for raw materials and for production facilities and equipment.

PREVENTION TECHNIQUES

- Use statistical quality control (SQC) techniques to ensure that costs are within a tolerable range.
- Use economic order quantity (EOQ) and material requirement planning (MRP) analysis for raw material ordering *(see Chapter 3:*

DEFICIENT INVENTORY BALANCES and EXCESSIVE ORDERING AND CARRYING COSTS).

- Make agreements with raw material suppliers for set prices and reliable delivery schedules; avoid multiple small orders where freight charges can cause costs to rise sharply.
- Create a more flexible cost budget. Cost planning allows the cost center to regulate how it spends money. Set early warning limits on expenditures to trigger a red flag before the cost goes out of control.
- Educate employees on the effects of inadequate cost control.
- Delegate certain employees to be watchdogs, monitoring yields and raw material usage. Teach them statistical process control (SPC) to help expedite the process for a product. SPC is a technique that helps estimate the probability that a production process is in control. This should help improve yields and maintain consistent product quality.

SPILLOVER EFFECTS

If costs cannot be controlled, it may be necessary to reduce staff and other operating expenditures to maintain profitability. Recapitalization may not be possible if money is lost due to poor cost control. If the cost control problem continues, diminished profitability, insolvency, and bankruptcy may be inevitable.

See also in this chapter: LACK OF COST INFORMATION, DISTORTED COST INFORMATION, and EXCESSIVE LABOR COSTS. In Chapter 4: UNPROFITABLE PROFIT CENTERS. In Chapter 5: LOW RATE OF RETURN.

PROBLEM
LACK OF COST INFORMATION
SYMPTOMS

- The accounting system provides incomplete or inaccurate cost data.
- Wrong financial decisions are being made based on unsupported or deficient data.

CAUSES

- Incompetent or inexperienced staff.
- Budget restrictions, resulting in a cutback in recording important costs, production management, and financial reports.
- Costs improperly classified in the records.
- Costs not broken down into variable and fixed costs, preventing breakeven and cost-volume-profit analysis.
- Failure to prepare detailed or adequate cost budgets.
- Use of an outdated cost accounting system that misstates the costs of products or services.

ANALYSIS

- Examine trend in costs over time.
- Set standards for costs.
- Compare budgeted to actual costs and investigate any deviation.
- Track fluctuations in costs.
- Examine the interrelationship among costs.

REPAIR

- Take inflation into account when estimating and analyzing costs.
- Hire competent cost accountants.
- Insist that personnel take courses in cost accounting.
- Modernize the cost accounting system, using JIT and activity-based costing (ABC). (ABC is a system that looks at activities as the fundamental cost objects.)
- Allocate costs to divisions and departments.

PREVENTION TECHNIQUES

- Hire an experienced consultant to identify weaknesses in the cost accounting system and recommend areas for improvement.
- Computerize the cost accounting system to incorporate the latest technological developments.
- Use up-to-date quantitative techniques to track costs.
- Have departmental managers identify cost information they feel they need but are not getting. Managers should take an active part in the budgeting and cost accounting process because they have an intimate knowledge of matters affecting their particular operations.

- Have costs managed by responsibility centers at the lowest level practical.
- Base prices for internal transfers of assembled products or services on a negotiated market value.
- Conduct a continuous internal audit of the cost accounting system to correct weaknesses as they arise.

SPILLOVER EFFECTS

If cost information is inadequate, the business cannot control its costs because it may not know the actual costs incurred by each responsibility center. Cost overruns decrease company profitability. By understating expenses, the company may be selling products for less than it costs to produce them. Bid prices on contracts may also be understated, causing operating losses. Managers who are not aware of actual operating costs incurred cannot plan adequately.

See also in this chapter: DISTORTED COST INFORMATION.

PROBLEM
DISTORTED COST INFORMATION
SYMPTOMS

- Loss of competitiveness in the marketplace.
- Loss of contract bids due to inaccurate product pricing.
- Loss of contribution due to poor product mix.
- Hard-to-explain outcomes of bids and profit margins.
- Surprisingly high profits on products or services that are difficult to produce.
- A desire by managers to drop products or services that appear profitable.
- No complaints from customers about price increases.
- Misleadingly high or low product prices.

CAUSES

- Wrong calculations for variable and fixed costs.
- One product carrying more of the fixed costs than others.

ANALYSIS

Many companies use a traditional cost system, such as job-order costing or process costing or a hybrid of the two. This traditional system may distort product cost information so that companies selling multiple products make critical decisions about product pricing, bidding, or product mix based on inaccurate cost data.

Usually the problem is not with assigning direct labor or materials costs. These prime costs are traceable to individual products, and most conventional cost systems are designed to ensure that they are traced. However, the assignment of overhead costs to individual products is another matter. Using the traditional methods of assigning overhead costs to products—using a single predetermined overhead rate based on any single activity measure—can distort product costs.

REPAIR

Use ABC with multiple cost drivers. (A *cost driver* is the basis for allocating a cost to a department.) Cost drivers that indirectly measure the consumption of an activity usually measure the number of transactions associated with that activity. It is possible to replace a cost driver that directly measures consumption with one that measures it only indirectly without loss of accuracy, provided that the quantities of activity consumed per transaction are stable for each product. Examples of cost drivers are direct labor hours, square footage of space, and number of orders placed.

PREVENTION TECHNIQUES

The financial manager needs to carefully evaluate cost drivers in designing a product costing system. A system using multiple cost drivers is more expensive to implement and use, but it may save millions.

- Use ABC to provide more accurate information about product costs and to help managers make better decisions about product design, pricing, marketing, and mix; ABC encourages continual operating improvements.
- Use a JIT costing system to convert indirect to direct costs. This conversion reduces the need to use multiple cost drivers to assign overhead costs to products, thus enhancing product-costing accuracy. For example, under the JIT system, workers on the production line do plant maintenance and setups, while under traditional

systems these activities were done by other workers classified as indirect labor. JIT, coupled with ABC, can greatly improve costing accuracy.

- Confirm total fixed costs and assign the proper fixed cost per unit to the product before releasing it to the market.
- Produce prototype products to determine the expected yield to establish the cost of the product.

SPILLOVER EFFECTS

Inaccuracies in calculating overhead cost per unit can lead to poor decisions about pricing, product mix, or contract bidding.

If the cost distortion is high, the product may be overpriced. High-priced products may be less price-competitive and have lower sales than expected. If the cost distortion is too high, the product may be considered too expensive to produce. If the cost distortion is too low, the product can lose profits for the company and even fail to achieve breakeven. Losses or loss products may force the company to reduce staff or facility size. In either case, lost business can hurt the company's future.

See also in this chapter: LACK OF COST INFORMATION.

PROBLEM
SUPPLIES MORE EXPENSIVE
OR UNAVAILABLE

SYMPTOMS

- Manufacturing delays.
- Low stocking of supplies and raw materials.
- Supplier strikes.
- Actual costs exceeding budgeted costs.
- Cash flow deficiencies.
- Failure to meet customer orders.

CAUSES

- Strikes at suppliers.
- Political unrest.
- Inflation or economic uncertainty.
- Poor materials planning.
- Inaccurate forecasts and budgets.

ANALYSIS

- Determine whether the business is overdependent on unreliable sources of supply.
- Examine past delivery problems with suppliers.
- Evaluate the trend in the ratio of raw material costs to sales over 10 years.
- Appraise the trend in the company's production over time and identify reasons for variances.

REPAIR

- Increase selling prices.
- Seek alternative sources of supplies.
- Substitute cheaper raw materials.
- Improve production efficiency.
- Initiate legal action if a contractual agreement has been violated.

PREVENTION TECHNIQUES

- Stock up on raw materials.
- Enter into futures contracts for delivery at a later date at a set price.
- Self-manufacture certain components.
- Enter into long-term supply arrangements.
- Acquire the supplier.
- Review trade publications for problems likely to arise externally.
- Use vertical integration to reduce the price and supply risks of raw materials.

SPILLOVER EFFECTS

- Profitability will decrease unless selling prices are also increased.
- Cash flow will diminish because of higher costs.
- Production cutbacks will be necessary, lowering sales volume for the product.
- Dissatisfied customers may shift to competitors.
- There will be higher risk and uncertainty regarding future earnings.

See in Chapter 4: EXCESSIVE COST IN RELATION TO PRODUCTION VOLUME.

PROBLEM
COST REDUCTIONS HAMPERING DEVELOPMENT

SYMPTOMS

- Declining sales.
- Loss of customers.
- Diminishing profitability.
- Layoffs and reduction of costs needed for future survival.

CAUSES

- Lack of good cost information.
- Postponement of necessary major repairs and upkeep.
- Failure to take into account the benefits of projected expenditures.
- Poor economy or business conditions.
- Deficient financial planning.
- Failure to analyze costs properly.
- Nonproductive assets and personnel.

ANALYSIS

The trend in the ratio of cost cuts to total costs will reveal the extent of the austerity program. Costs and sales should also be compared over several periods, with special attention to revenue lost because of cost reduction programs (market share lost, for example, because of failure to advertise).

REPAIR

- Better cost analysis to determine the benefits derived from incurring certain costs.
- Cost management to assure that costs are at the minimal without adversely affecting business.

PREVENTION TECHNIQUES

- Determine exactly where costs can be cut with minimal adverse financial consequences.
- Hire an independent consultant.
- Make more use of budget and financial models.

SPILLOVER EFFECTS

- Long-term decline in profitability.
- Lower growth rate.
- Failure to maintain a competitive position because of inability to promote product or service innovations.
- Erosion of the customer base.
- Failure to maintain up-to-date accounting records.

See also in this chapter: EXCESSIVE LABOR COSTS *and* REDUCED DISCRETIONARY COSTS HURTING THE BUSINESS.

PROBLEM
REDUCED DISCRETIONARY COSTS HURTING THE BUSINESS

SYMPTOMS

A reduction in spending on advertising, repairs and maintenance, research and development, and training.

CAUSE

The business has not properly analyzed the benefits of these discretionary investments.

ANALYSIS

Analysts should determine the trends in:

- Discretionary costs as a percentage of net sales.
- Discretionary costs to the assets with which they are associated.

Declining trends may presage future deterioration in operations. For example, a declining trend in repairs and maintenance costs as a percentage of fixed assets may indicate failure to maintain capital facilities.

Index numbers may be used to compare current discretionary expenditures with base-year expenditures. An index number is simply a ratio of a current-year amount to a base-year amount. The base year should be a year that is fairly typical.

Ask whether the current level of discretionary costs is consistent with previous trends and with the company's present and future requirements.

REPAIR

Reinstate realistic discretionary costs.

PREVENTION TECHNIQUE

Before cutting costs, analyze the long-term financial and operational effects of doing so.

SPILLOVER EFFECTS

- Failure to keep abreast of current developments.
- Breakdown of machinery, leading to production curtailments.
- Improperly trained staff.
- Decreased market share.
- Failure to develop new products.
- Deterioration in employee morale.
- Loss of business to competitors.
- Long-term decline in corporate profitability and earning power.

See also in this chapter: COST REDUCTIONS HAMPERING DEVELOPMENT.

PROBLEM
UP-FRONT COSTS IMPEDING PROJECT AUTHORIZATION

SYMPTOMS

- Significant outlay of expenditures.
- High percentage of projects rejected because of high startup costs.

CAUSES

- Inadequate financial planning.
- Deficient financial position, including low liquidity, failure to obtain financing, and deficient budgeting.

ANALYSIS

- Examine the ratio of up-front costs to total costs of a proposed project.
- Compare budgeted to actual costs.

- Compare the number of projects rejected because of high initial costs to total projects.

REPAIR

- Plan for adequate funding for projects from debt or equity sources, or both.
- Set up a joint venture with another business.
- Get venture capital financing by selling equity interest.
- Sell assets to raise cash.

PREVENTION TECHNIQUES

- Better planning at the proposal stage.
- Open lines of credit.
- Postponing expenditures to the extent possible.
- Dividing large projects into smaller self-contained units.
- Joining with other companies that have a successful record of product and service innovation.

SPILLOVER EFFECTS

- Lower earnings potential and growth.
- Inability to issue more stock because prospective investors view the business as a poor risk because it lacks growth potential.
- A competitive disadvantage because of lack of innovative projects.

PROBLEM
PRICING LOWERING PROFITS

SYMPTOM

Sales lead to lower profits even though cost is minimized and the optimal quantity is produced and sold.

CAUSE

Raising prices cannot offset the cost of selling to slow-paying customers.

ANALYSIS

Calculate the price elasticity of demand of the product or service. Price elasticity, denoted with e_p, is the ratio of a percentage change in quantity demanded (Q) to a percentage change in price (p).

$$e_p = \frac{dQ/Q}{dp/p} = \frac{dQ}{dp} \times \frac{P}{Q}$$

where dQ/dp is simply the slope of the demand function Q = (p). We classify price elasticity demand in three categories:

If $e_p > 1$, elastic.
$e_p = 1$, unitary.
$e_p < 1$, inelastic.

Example: The demand function is given as Q = 200 - 6p. The price elasticity at p = 4 is computed as follows:
First,

$$Q = 200 - 6(4) = 176.$$

Since dQ/dp = -6, the e_p at p = 4 is:

$$e_p = -6 \times \left(\frac{4}{176}\right) = -0.136$$

This means that a 1 percent change in price will bring about a 0.14 percent change in demand. The product under study is considered price inelastic, because the e_p is less than 1 in absolute value.

Economists have established the relationships shown in Table 6.1 between price elasticity (e_p) and total revenue (TR) that can help a firm set prices.

TABLE 6.1. PRICES AND ELASTICITY OF DEMAND

Price	$e_p > 1$	$e_p = 1$	$e_p < 1$
Price rises	TR falls	No change	TRrises
Price falls	TR rises	No change	TR falls

Firms must be aware of the elasticity of the demand curves for their own products when they set product prices.

A profit-maximizing company would never choose to lower prices in the inelastic range of its demand curve. That would only decrease total revenue while also increasing costs, since output would be rising. The result would be a drastic decrease in profits. In fact, when costs are rising and the product is inelastic, the firm would have no difficulty passing on the increased costs by raising the price.

On the other hand, when there are many substitutes and demand is quite elastic, increasing prices may reduce rather than increase total revenue. The result may be lower rather than higher profits.

While the goal of virtually all companies is to increase market share, the marketing strategy required to maximize profits is to determine the optimal price. Companies need to focus on being profitable rather than on increasing sales dollars. They must examine whether their pricing strategies are effective. Two of the most important pricing strategies are:

1. *Premium pricing*, which should result in a higher percentage return than the return on the standard model.
2. *Marginal pricing*, which is appropriate when a company has an advantage over its competitors.

A pricing strategy that maximizes profits must be in place before a product is introduced, and the price must be adjusted according to demand.

REPAIR

- Base pricing on market demand.
- Do test-market analysis.

PREVENTION TECHNIQUES

Pricing decisions must be made in light of their likely short-term and long-term effects on the enterprise. Accept short-term orders for less than factory costs if there is excess capacity and if the selling price quoted would cover the variable costs (a positive contribution margin).

SPILLOVER EFFECTS

- Poor pricing policies lower profits.
- Accepting too many low-price special orders may drive down the market price.
- Decreases in average unit price will distort the figures used in breakeven analyses, requiring that they be recalculated.
- A decrease in EPS decrease will cause a decrease in the value of the company.
- A company that fails to operate at an acceptable profit level will face possible insolvency and bankruptcy.

See in Chapter 11: HIGHER PRICES REDUCING SALES *and* LOWER PRICES SHRINKING MARGINS.

Chapter 7
Financing Undermining Business Development

A company may experience significant financial problems that adversely affect the market price of its stocks and bonds. Its credit and bond ratings may deteriorate. It may be unable to obtain financing at reasonable rates and terms. Inability to issue new securities and negotiate loans starves the business of the funds it needs to operate. If loan provisions are violated, bankers may force the business into liquidation. If dividends are restricted because of a lack of cash, stockholders may decide to replace corporate management.

In this chapter, we look at the following problems:
- Falling market price of stock.
- Drop in bond rating.
- Inability to obtain financing.
- Inability to issue new securities.
- Dividends restricted.
- Restrictive loan agreements breached.

PROBLEM
MARKET PRICE OF STOCK FALLING

SYMPTOMS

- There is less demand for the company's shares.
- Brokers recommend that investors sell or avoid buying the stock.
- Poor reviews of the company appear in the financial press.
- The company is the target of a takeover attempt.
- The market value of the company's common stock is below its book value.
- Lenders place stringent credit requirements on the company.
- Financing costs are increasing.
- Previous sources of financing are no longer available.

CAUSES

- Market conditions.
- Excessive business risk.
- Poor management.
- Continuous operating losses.
- Inconsistent earnings performance.
- Negative future economic developments expected in the company's line of business.
- Foreign competition.
- Government action.
- Loss of key managerial personnel.
- Cash flow problems.
- A generally deficient financial position.
- Poor return on stockholder equity.
- Profit expectations not met.
- Failure to keep up with new technological or with market conditions.

ANALYSIS

- Determine the percentage drop in the market price of stock over time.
- Chart price changes to see their general direction and movements.
- Identify times during the year when the stock price seems especially vulnerable.

- Compare the change in the market price of the stock to that of competing companies, the industry, and major stock indexes.
- Chart the P/E ratio (stock price divided by EPS) over time and compare it with the industry P/E ratio.

REPAIR

- Have company buy back its own shares.
- Improve earnings and financial position.
- Diversify to reduce risk.
- Issue preferred stock and bonds so as not to further dilute the market price of common stock.
- Issue securities privately rather than publicly.
- Have the board of directors issue a reverse stock split to increase price per share.
- Establish dividend reinvestment programs employee stock option plans, and issue stock rights to existing stockholders.

PREVENTION TECHNIQUES

- Meet with security analysts to explain positive financial aspects of the company.
- Give interviews to reporters for financial newspapers so that they understand the favorable situation of the company.
- Deny false rumors promptly.
- Hire an investment banker to advise about improving share price.

SPILLOVER EFFECTS

- Management may be voted out of office.
- The sale of shares of the company's stock may be accelerated, causing a further drop in the market price.
- The cost of financing may increase because of the perceived deterioration in the company's financial position.
- There are fewer sources of funds.
- The company may have to reorganize or be liquidated.
- Stock options held by executives and employees may be worth less.
- The company may appear to the average or unsophisticated investor to be a poor investment.

See also in this chapter: DROP IN BOND RATING. *In Chapter 2*: POOR CREDIT RATING. *In Chapter 5:*INADEQUATE LIQUIDITY, INSOLVENCY, UNSTABLE OPERATIONS AND EARNINGS, LOW PRICE/EARNINGS RATIO, *and* POOR PROFITABILITY AND GROWTH.

PROBLEM
DROP IN BOND RATING

SYMPTOMS

- Company fails to make interest payments or to pay creditors and suppliers.
- Financial advisory services place the company on credit watch lists.
- Credit reporting services downgrade the company's bond rating.

CAUSES

- Inability to make interest payments.
- Lack of consistent performance.
- Higher debt/equity ratio.
- Declining working capital and cash flow position.
- Poor balance-sheet posture.

ANALYSIS

- Evaluate the financial statement and the overall performance of the enterprise.
- Conduct horizontal, vertical, and ratio analysis.
- Calculate trend percentages (a form of horizontal analysis).
- Study the reports of business publications to determine external opinion of the company as an investment vehicle.
- Review brokerage research reports.
- Compare the company's operating figures with industry norms and competitors.
- Study the company's cash flow statement.
- Calculate the liquidity and profitability ratios, which reflect the company's ability to pay current liabilities and long-term debt.

REPAIR

- Ask the bond credit rating services what financial procedures they would prefer to see your company initiate to reverse the downgrade.
- If possible, institute their recommendations and inform both the rating services and the investing public of your intention to improve the company's performance.
- If the current market interest rate has dropped, redeem existing bonds and issue new debt at the lower market rate.
- Issue bonds that have a conversion feature that enables holders to convert the bonds into either preferred or common stock at a time when the creditors consider it profitable to do so.
- Renegotiate a lower interest rate with lenders.
- Issue stock at a favorable price to bring in equity funds so as to lower the debt/equity ratio.
- Sell assets to pay debt.
- Use tangible assets as collateral for the sale of bonds.
- Establish a maximum debt ceiling that cannot be exceeded.

PREVENTION TECHNIQUES

- Reduce costs.
- Sell off assets.
- Diversify to reduce risk.
- Lengthen the maturity dates of bonds.
- Keep credit reporting agencies informed of the company's financial situation and plans.
- Defer the payment of loans for a year.
- Offer creditors the opportunity to convert the debt into stock at a favorable conversion rate.
- Plan for future conditions in the economy and the money market.
- Do not overextend the company, either financially or operationally.
- Hedge by matching maturity dates of debt to collection or maturity date of assets.

SPILLOVER EFFECTS

A downward bond rating will make it more difficult to borrow, which will increase interest costs. These increased costs will negatively affect earnings and cash flow.

See also in this chapter: MARKET PRICE OF STOCK FALLING. *In Chapter 2:* POOR CREDIT RATING. *In Chapter 5:* EXCESSIVE DEBT.

PROBLEM
INABILITY TO OBTAIN FINANCING
SYMPTOMS

- Loan applications refused.
- Line of credit limited.
- Inability to attract buyers for bonds and stock.
- Financing available only at exorbitant interest rates.
- Significant restrictions on loans.
- Company assets pledged as collateral for loans.

CAUSES

- Inadequate liquid reserves.
- Increased risk of insolvency.
- Obsolete assets.
- Poor earnings.
- Excessive business risks.
- A weak economy.

ANALYSIS

Failure to obtain financing may be evaluated by examining:
- The trend in financing obtained by source.
- The ratio of loan applications denied to total loan applications.
- The trend in the effective interest rate (interest divided by loan proceeds).
- Declines in the market price of the company's bonds and stocks.
- A drop in bond ratings.
- The trend for increased collateralization of assets.

A higher ratio of sales to accounts payable indicates that the company is unable to obtain short-term credit in the form of cost-free funds to finance sales growth.

REPAIR

To obtain financing the company must:
• Provide sufficient collateral.
• Sell an equity interest in the business.
• Agree to higher interest rates and loan restrictions.
• Factor or assign receivables.
• Sell or shut down unprofitable divisions or subsidiaries.

PREVENTION TECHNIQUES

• Obtain open lines of credit from banks.
• Repay all loans promptly.
• Improve the company's financial position through cost cutting and layoffs.
• Cease production of unprofitable products or services.
• Lease assets instead of buying them.
• Extend and stagger payment dates of liabilities.
• Avoid excessive debt.
• Note loan restrictions the company may be in danger of violating.
• Compare the current status of all loans to all loan compliance requirements to determine to what extent there is a safety buffer.
• Plan for likely future conditions in the economy and the money market.

SPILLOVER EFFECTS

• Deteriorating cash position.
• Increased cost of capital.
• Higher compensating balances required.
• Increased business risk.
• Financial instability.
• Lower credit rating.
• Bankruptcy, if the business cannot obtain credit to meet its financial obligations.

See in Chapter 5: INADEQUATE LIQUIDITY.

PROBLEM
INABILITY TO ISSUE NEW SECURITIES
SYMPTOMS

- Investors refuse to buy new issues of common stock, preferred stock, or bonds.
- Prices of existing securities drop significantly.
- Lenders place stringent credit requirements on the company.
- Financing costs increase.
- Previous sources of financing are no longer available.

CAUSES

- Market conditions.
- Excessive business risk.
- Poor management.
- Continuous operating losses.
- Likely negative future economic developments in the company's line of business.
- Increased foreign competition.
- Government action.
- Excessive interest and labor costs.
- Overexpansion or diversification into areas where the company has no experience.
- Cash flow problems.
- A generally deficient financial position.
- Lowered stock and bond ratings.

ANALYSIS

Examine the trend in the following ratios over the years and compare the company's ratios to those of competing companies and industry averages:

- Funds obtained from new bond financing to total liabilities.
- Funds obtained from new stock financing to total stockholder equity.

REPAIR

- Give up some control of the company to obtain funds.
- Try to place securities privately rather than publicly.

- Negotiate with venture capital groups.
- Provide collateral for financing.
- Seek out alternative financing strategies.
- Obtain open lines of credit from banks.
- Establish joint ventures with other companies to obtain financing.
- Offer higher financial incentives to investment bankers to encourage them to deal in the company's securities.
- Try to obtain government grants.
- Seek export financing in foreign countries.
- Delay capital expenditures.

PREVENTION TECHNIQUES

- Issue convertible exchangeable preferred stock that allows the company to force conversion from convertible preferred stock into convertible debt.
- Issue participating preferred stock that allows shareholders to participate above the stated yield of the stock.
- Issue floating rate preferred stock.
- Offer Dutch auction preferred stock, in which the shares are reauctioned every seven weeks.
- Establish an employee stock ownership plan (ESOP) to place shares and votes in the friendly hands of employees.
- Issue new equity shares with preemptive rights.
- Institute an installment sales procedure to issue new securities over a stated period of time rather than all at once in one large offering.
- Time the issuance of new stocks and bonds to coincide with improving economic and market conditions.
- Issue shares in bull markets and refrain from issuing them in bear markets.
- Offer higher-yielding common stock just before the ax-dividend date so that investors will be attracted to it.
- Improve internal generation of funds (cash flow from operations) so that there is less reliance on external financing.
- Improve the company's financial position through cost reduction and restructuring.

- Stretch repayment dates on bond issues.
- Apply to federal loan programs.

SPILLOVER EFFECTS

Inability to issue new securities may create cash flow and operating problems:
- Increased cost of capital.
- Higher compensating balances required.
- Increased business risk.
- Financial instability.
- Bankruptcy, if business cannot obtain credit to meet its financial obligations.

If financing does become available, it may be at high risk and on very restrictive terms. The restrictions will inhibit the freedom of action of financial managers.

A firm with a lower credit rating and low share price may also become a candidate for takeover.

See also in this chapter: DROP IN BOND RATING *and* INABILITY TO OBTAIN FINANCING. *In Chapter 1:* CASH OUTFLOWS EXCEEDING CASH INFLOWS *and* INADEQUATE CASH POSITION. *In Chapter 5:* EXCESSIVE DEBT, INADEQUATE WORKING CAPITAL, INSOLVENCY, *and* POOR PROFITABILITY AND GROWTH. *In Chapter 13:* INABILITY TO REPAY DEBT *and* BANKRUPTCY ON THE HORIZON.

PROBLEM
DIVIDENDS RESTRICTED

SYMPTOMS

- Cash flow problems.
- Failure to generate earnings sufficient to pay a cash dividend.
- Insolvency.
- Loan agreements that restrict the payment of dividends because a certain level of profits has not been attained.
- Attempts to dismiss management by unhappy stockholders.

CAUSES

- Insolvency.
- Earnings too low to pay a cash dividend.
- Urgent need (especially in rapidly growing businesses) for substantial funds to reinvest or finance investment opportunities.
- Intentional failure to pay dividends because a majority of the shareholders are in a high marginal tax bracket (especially where the company is closely held).
- Agreements in bond covenants that require that a portion of the company's earnings be set aside as additional protection for creditors.
- State laws requiring that accumulated earnings be restricted to an amount equal to the cost of treasury shares acquired.
- Management desire to plow earnings back into financial growth or expansion.
- Management decision to smooth out yearly dividend payments by accumulating earnings in profitable years and paying them out in years when there is an operating loss.
- A policy of building up cash as a buffer against possible changes in the tax law or accounting rules, future tax audits, or operating losses.

ANALYSIS

Dividends are payable only from funds legally available for such purposes under the law of the state of incorporation. Dividend *yield* (dividends per share/market price per share) is a measure of the current return to an investor in a stock. The yield will drop if the corporation reduces or fails to pay a cash dividend for a given period of time.

Study the P/E ratio. When the P/E ratio is higher than the P/E ratios of other companies, it usually signifies potential for increased earnings and investor confidence because they expect high dividends and growth. On the other hand, a lower P/E ratio is usually the result of a negative assessment by investors.

Payment of a stock dividend may also hide the inability of management to generate cash flow, a possibility that sophisticated investors would consider negative.

REPAIR

- Prepare a cash forecast to see whether the company can lift the restriction on payment of cash dividends.
- Analyze the expansion requirements of the corporation.
- Attempt to maintain a pattern of consistent dividend payment.
- Renegotiate agreements in bond covenants with specific creditors to reduce the amount that must be set aside as additional protection for creditors.

PREVENTION TECHNIQUES

- Pay a stock dividend or offer a stock split.
- Sell off unproductive assets or borrow funds to pay a cash dividend.

SPILLOVER EFFECTS

Nonpayment of or a reduction in company's dividend payout ratio will depress the stock price. An added concern for a closely held company is how changing dividends will affect stockholder personal tax liabilities.

PROBLEM
RESTRICTIVE LOAN AGREEMENTS BREACHED

SYMPTOMS

- Excessive debt.
- Indications in a financial report that management has ignored the ratios or limitations it agreed to.
- Threats by creditors to demand payment of the entire amount outstanding, or to force the company into bankruptcy unless management reduces the outstanding debt, meets the agreed ratios, or rescinds any unauthorized transactions.

CAUSES

- Demand for additional cash by management.
- Failure of management to adhere to restraints in company loan agreements.

- Misinterpretation or ignorance of the covenants in the loan agreements.

ANALYSIS

Bondholders and other long-term creditors may exercise control through protective covenants in a loan agreement. Typical covenants are:

- A lower limit on the company's current ratio.
- A minimum working capital requirement.
- An upper limit on the company's debt/equity ratio.
- A requirement that the enterprise not acquire or sell major assets over a stated amount without creditor approval.
- A requirement that total loans shall not exceed a stated amount.

REPAIR

- Hire a lawyer and a CPA to review all loan agreements.
- Have the accounting staff or outside auditors review the financial statements to make sure they have been prepared correctly.
- Review the safety buffer between loan requirement and actual financial status.
- Build a professional and friendly relationship with the bank.
- Review all financial statements for accurate recording of liabilities.
- Sell assets or issue additional shares of stock to pay off high-interest loans.
- Renegotiate loan restrictions to achieve greater flexibility in operations.
- Offer to exchange outstanding loan obligations for stock of the enterprise.

PREVENTION TECHNIQUES

- Reduce borrowing.
- Raise funds by issuing more stock.
- Bring in additional partners to provide funds.

SPILLOVER EFFECTS

Increased loan interest costs or unavailability of financing may lead to excessive fixed costs and bankruptcy. The sale of stock may result in loss of control over the enterprise.

Chapter 8
Risk Overshadows Return

There is a tradeoff between risk and return. The higher the risk, the greater should be the return. Managing working capital (current assets less current liabilities) involves this tradeoff. If funds change from fixed assets to current assets, the company reduces its liquidity risk and increases its flexibility and its ability to obtain short-term financing. The change also enables the company to quickly adjust current assets to changes in sales volume. But the return is less because the yield on fixed assets is generally more than that of current assets. Financing with noncurrent debt has less liquidity risk than financing with current debt, but long-term debt often has a higher cost than short-term debt because of the greater uncertainty, which detracts from the overall return.

There are many corporate risks. For example, a company may be overly dependent on a few employees or on government contracts, or there may be a militant union. It may be operating in politically and economically unstable foreign countries. It may have to meet complex and burdensome environmental and safety regulations.

Many of the risks facing a business can be reduced, prevented, or eliminated because they are to some degree controllable by management. For example, inflation risk may be minimized by pricing ahead of inflation on a next-in, first-out basis, so that the selling price is based on the expected replacement cost of the item. In many cases, risk can be reduced through diversification in the product or service line, geographically, and in investments. Sometimes, unfortunately, risk is not minimized due to a lack of communication within the organization. The following problems are discussed in this chapter:

* Risk disproportionate to return.
* Risk in the industry.
* Risk in corporate operations.
* Lack of diversification.
* Inflationary risk.
* Political risk.
* Foreign exchange risk.
* Social and environmental risks.
* Management unaware of financial problems.

PROBLEM
RISK DISPROPORTIONATE TO RETURN
SYMPTOMS

* Difficulty meeting debt payments.
* Lower ratings on stocks and bonds.
* Inability to borrow or raise money on favorable terms.

CAUSES

* Too much use of financial leverage (other people's money).
* Higher operating leverage caused by large fixed costs.
* High debt/equity ratio.
* High beta (the percentage change in the market price of a stock relative to the percentage change in the price of a stock index like the Standard & Poor's 500).

ANALYSIS

The financial manager must compare the expected return for a given financial decision with the kind of risk it carries. There are six types of risk:

1. *Business risk* is the risk that the company will have general business problems, such as changes in demand, input prices, and obsolescence due to technological advances.
2. *Liquidity risk* represents the possibility that it may not be possible to sell an asset on short notice for its market value. An invest-

ment that must be sold at a high discount is said to have substantial liquidity risk.

3. *Default risk* is the risk that the company cannot make interest or principal repayments on debt.

4. *Market risk* refers to changes in the price of a stock that result from changes in the stock market as a whole, regardless of the company's earning power.

5. *Interest rate risk* refers to fluctuations in the value of an asset as interest rates and conditions set by the money and capital markets change. Interest rate risk relates to fixed-income securities, such as bonds and real estate.

6. *Purchasing power risk* relates to the possibility of receiving less for an asset than was originally invested, taking inflation into account.

REPAIR

• Monitor fixed discretionary operating costs (such as advertising and R&D).

• Pay off high-interest debts or exchange them for equity shares.

PREVENTION TECHNIQUES

• Rebalance the company's financing mix.

• Finance on favorable terms.

• Ensure that the company adheres to the five Cs (1) character, (2) cash flow, (3) capital, (4) collateral, and (5) economic condition.

• Keep bond ratings in a respectable category.

SPILLOVER EFFECTS

• A decline in the market value of the company, possibly resulting in bankruptcy.

• Difficulty obtaining financing on favorable terms.

• Downgraded credit and bond ratings.

See also in this chapter: RISK IN CORPORATE OPERATIONS. *In Chapter 2*: POOR CREDIT RATING. *In Chapter 5:* LOW RATE OF RETURN. *In Chapter 7*: DROP IN BOND RATING.

PROBLEM
RISK IN THE INDUSTRY
SYMPTOMS

Throughout the industry there are signs of contraction, turbulence, and vulnerability, as evidenced in:

* Declining sales and profitability.
* High managerial turnover.
* Overreliance on energy and consequent vulnerability to an energy shortage.
* Stringent governmental and environmental regulation and unfavorable tax rules.
* Consistently low marks in the Wall Street Journal and Barron's.
* Continuous consumer lawsuits relating to product quality, performance, or environmental hazards.
* A negative public image.
* Growing vulnerability to new and improved products from both domestic and foreign competition.

CAUSES

* There is excessive competition or a limited number of companies control a high percentage of the market.
* Companies in the industry cannot raise prices enough to meet increasing costs.
* The industry is technologically oriented and is having trouble keeping up to date.
* Companies in the industry are capital-intensive, with a record of cyclical performance.

ANALYSIS

* Appraise the industry cycle.
* Evaluate the past and projected stability of the industry.

REPAIR

* Diversify by acquiring companies in growing or countercyclical industries.
* Acquire or merge with one or more competing companies.

- Move toward a labor-intensive business because it is easier to lay off employees in recessionary times than it is to reduce investment in plant and equipment.
- Move toward a staple-product business for greater earnings stability.

PREVENTION TECHNIQUES

- Diversify by acquiring companies in different industries or branching out into other product and service areas.
- Engage in joint ventures with other companies.
- Vertically integrate with energy suppliers.
- Cut product and service costs.
- Institute an advertising campaign to promote the industry's image.
- Settle consumer lawsuits out of court and establish a committee to review the causes of these actions.
- Lobby for legislation favorable to the industry.

SPILLOVER EFFECTS

Companies in an unhealthy industry tend to perform poorly. Excessive competition may result in declining profits and insolvency. The industry will lag in the stock market.

See also in this chapter: POLITICAL RISK.

PROBLEM
RISK IN CORPORATE OPERATIONS

SYMPTOMS

- Operations and earnings are unstable and consistently unprofitable.
- The company faces lawsuits for defective products, sexual harassment, or other major causes.
- Upper management is unaware of current or potential operating problems.
- The company has been the target of consumer boycotts and governmental intervention.
- It has contractual disputes with unions and other companies.

- The government is disputing certain contract costs and is seeking to renegotiate contracts.
- There are problems with the Internal Revenue Service.
- Turnover of experienced and valuable employees is high.
- Production quotas and schedules are not being met.
- Sales orders are not being filled because completed inventory is not available for immediate shipment.
- Costs are not being monitored.
- Internal control procedures are inadequate.

CAUSES

- Overdependence on a few key executives, unreliable suppliers, and a few large customers.
- Improper hiring and training of employees.
- Lack of a well-defined corporate ethics and behavior policy.
- Products and services that are susceptible to rapid technological change and obsolescence.

ANALYSIS

- Compare the company's risk exposure to its own past record and that of other companies in the industry.
- Use beta to measure the company's risk relative to the market. A beta greater than 1 means risk, because the company's stock vacillates more than the average.
- Evaluate labor quiescence by determining the number and duration of previous strikes, the degree of union militancy, and employee turnover.
- Calculate operating and financial leverage. (Operating leverage is the percentage change in earnings before tax and interest to the percentage change in sales. Financial leverage is the ratio of total debt to total equity.)

REPAIR

- Strengthen the executive base.
- Change suppliers who prove unreliable.
- Diversify the customer base.
- Seek to improve labor relations.
- Improve communications between senior and operating managers.

- Settle disputes with governmental agencies as quickly as possible.
- Evaluate internal control procedures for recording expenses.

PREVENTION TECHNIQUES

- Diversify products and investments.
- Move into new domestic and international markets (but only if you have adequate expertise).
- Acquire a successful company to obtain experienced management, new channels of distribution, sources of supply, economies of scale, and a broader customer base.
- Diversify the current customer and supplier base.
- Work out a negative correlation between products and services.
- Enter countercyclical lines of business.
- Emphasize items with inelastic demand, which remains relatively stable (as with medicine) even though the price changes.
- Insure against all possible asset and operating losses.
- Improve hiring practices to obtain the most competent and productive employees.
- Establish employee programs that identify and cure the kind of employee behavior that might provoke lawsuits.
- Update employee skills.
- Improve community relations.
- Move operations geographically to minimize such environmental risks as floods.
- Improve and review tax-planning techniques.

SPILLOVER EFFECTS

- Operating losses.
- Lower market prices for stocks and bonds.
- More costly financing.
- Difficulty hiring qualified personnel.

See also in this chapter: RISK DISPROPORTIONATE TO RETURN, INFLATIONARY RISK, POLITICAL RISK, *and* RISK IN THE INDUSTRY. *In Chapter 5:* EXCESSIVE DEBT. *In Chapter 6:* EXCESSIVE OPERATING LEVERAGE.

PROBLEM
LACK OF DIVERSIFICATION
SYMPTOMS

- Increased risk.
- Highly specialized and concentrated operations.
- Lower profitability.
- Low return on the company investment portfolio.

CAUSES

- Overreliance on a single product, with consequent susceptibility to revenue fluctuation and product obsolescence.
- A product line with a high positive correlation and demand for all products moving in the same direction.
- Products with elastic demand, experiencing significant changes in quantity sold with modest changes in price.
- All company operations located in one geographic region and thus highly dependent on the economic and political context of that locality.
- An investment portfolio concentrated in securities issued by companies that are in the same industries.

ANALYSIS

In appraising a company's product line, determine:
- The *degree of correlation* between its products.
- The *elasticity of product* demand.

Correlation between products is revealed through a correlation matrix determined by computer. Elasticity of demand is measured by the percentage change in quantity sold associated with a percentage change in price. The following ratio is used:

$$\frac{\text{Percentage change in quantity sold}}{\text{Percentage change in price}}$$

If the ratio is greater than 1, demand is elastic. If it is exactly 1, demand is unitary. If the ratio is less than 1, demand is inelastic. *Risk* exists *when products are positively correlated and have elastic demands*, because demand for the products all moves in the same direction and product demand is significantly influenced by price changes.

Example 1: The correlation matrix of Company I's product line is shown in Table 8.1.

TABLE 8.1. SAMPLE CORRELATION MATRIX

Product	*A*	*B*	*C*	*D*	*E*	*F*
A	1.00	0.13	-0.02	-0.01	-0.07	0.22
B	0.13	1.00	-0.02	-0.07	0.00	0.00
C	-0.02	-0.02	1.00	0.01	0.48	0.13
D	-0.01	-0.07	0.01	1.00	0.01	-0.02
E	-0.07	0.00	0.48	0.01	1.00	0.45
F	0.22	0.00	0.13	-0.02	0.45	1.00

Of course, correlation with the same product is perfect—the correlation between product A and product A is 1.00.

There is high positive correlation between products E and C (0.48) and E and F (0.45). This indicates risk.

There is low negative correlation between products A and D (-0.01) and A and C (-0.02), and no correlation between products B and E (0.00) and B and F (0.00). It would be better for company I if it had some products that had significant negative correlations (i.e., -0.60). Unfortunately, it does not.

Example 2: The two major products of company J are X and Y:

	X	Y
Selling price per unit	$10.00	$8.00
Current sales in units	10,000	13,000

If the selling price of product X is increased to $1 1.00, sales volume will decrease by 500 units. If the selling price of product Y is increased to $9.50, sales volume will decrease by 4,000 units.

The elasticity of demand is:

$$\frac{\text{Percentage change in quantity sold}}{\text{Percentage change in price}}$$

Product X has inelastic demand:

$$\frac{500/10,000}{\$1/\$10} = \frac{0.05}{.010} = 0.5$$

Product Y has elastic demand:

$$\frac{4,000/13,000}{\$1.50/\$8.00} = \frac{0.307}{0.188} = 1.63$$

Besides analyzing the product line, it is also necessary to evaluate the degree of diversification and stability associated with the company's investment portfolio. Securities should be diversified by industry and economic sector.

REPAIR

- Immediately diversify by product line, geographic area, and investment security.
- Set up a strategic unit to develop a diversification plan.

PREVENTION TECHNIQUES

- Diversify the product line to reduce the range of results that stem from differing economic conditions.
- Acquire established operating companies selling profitable products.
- Move from products with elastic demand to those with inelastic demand to enhance stability in operations and reduce risk.
- Diversify geographically to reduce risk of economic declines. This may be done regionally (among states and cities) or internationally (among countries).
- Diversify the investment portfolio to increase its price stability. Add international investments to a portfolio of U. S. securities.

SPILLOVER EFFECTS

- Greater uncertainty.
- Decreased earning power.
- Deteriorating growth rate.
- More susceptibility to business cycle shocks.

PROBLEM
INFLATION RISK

SYMPTOMS

- Real earnings are declining even though profitability seems satisfactory.
- Assets are losing purchasing power or are being improperly managed.
- Costs are escalating beyond control.

CAUSES

- The company is not keeping abreast of inflation by increasing the prices of what it sells.
- Current prices for future deliveries are not guaranteed by futures contracts.
- Cost increases are not hedged.
- Monetary assets are losing purchasing power.
- The company is not taking advantage of monetary liabilities that result in purchasing power gains during inflationary periods.

ANALYSIS

Determine the impact of inflation on net income by comparing the consumer price index (CPI), adjusted net income, and current cost net income with reported earnings. If the amount reported in the income statement is materially higher than the other net income measures, the quality of earnings is poor—the wider the difference, the lower the quality of net income.

REPAIR

- Increase selling prices at short intervals to maintain adequate profit margins.
- Modify catalogues and sales literature to reflect increases in prices.
- Give price quotations good only for short periods of time (e.g., two months).
- Price on a next-in, first-out basis.
- Include the current cost of capital in the selling price.
- Price ahead of inflation.

- Provide for price increases when there are long lead times between receiving orders and shipping goods.
- Obtain partial payments as work is performed.
- Incorporate "cost-plus" provisions, possibly tied to the CPI, in long-term contracts.
- Enter into futures contracts to guarantee raw materials at currently lower prices.
- Restrict dividends to preserve earning power and retain needed cash.

PREVENTION TECHNIQUES

- Try to cut costs and improve efficiency.
- Substitute cheaper sources of supply or self-manufacture certain parts.
- Make long-term purchase agreements and encourage suppliers to quote firm prices.
- Look for suppliers who offer beneficial credit terms.
- Obtain competitive bids from insurance companies and periodically change carriers to secure the lowest premiums.
- Redesign the delivery system to reduce fuel costs.
- De-emphasize inflation-resistant products.
- Avoid responding to proposals that require significant investments and have long payback periods.
- Tie salary increments to increased productivity.
- Keep cash and receivables at minimum balances to protect against a purchasing power loss.
- Use debt to gain purchasing power (because payments are made to creditors in cheaper dollars).
- Make investments in areas requiring minimal expenditures and short lead times.
- Use accounting methods that reduce taxable income in order to minimize tax payments.

SPILLOVER EFFECTS

Failure to reduce inflation risk will erode the company's purchasing power. In real dollars, the company is experiencing a diminishing economic position. This will have an adverse effect on earnings, cash flow, and the company's stock price.

PROBLEM
POLITICAL RISK

SYMPTOMS

- Long-term investments abroad.
- Stringent government requirements.

CAUSES

- Domestic spending on contracts and government subsidies is vulnerable to changing political realities.
- Agricultural enterprises are hurt by commodity embargoes.
- Government regulations are very stringent, tying up financial management's options.
- The company is vulnerable to current and proposed legislation that will increase its taxes.
- A local regulatory body is hostile to the company.
- A utility's request for a rate increase is denied or delayed.
- There is a war in regions where there is high U. S. investment.

ANALYSIS

Businesses tend to make long-term investments in foreign countries. Since it may take a long period of time to recover the initial investment, companies do not expect to liquidate their initial investment quickly. This situation can produce difficulties in repatriating funds from a foreign country when the ruling government has changed dramatically.

Compounding these difficulties are currency fluctuations and restrictive local customs and regulations. For example, a U. S. company doing business in Japan may be unable to fire employees, making labor a fixed cost. There are also variations in tax laws, balance of payments policies, and government controls on types and sizes of investments, as well as types of capital raised. Government may control wages, the selling price of the product or service, and local borrowing.

Stringent national and local environmental and safety regulations may govern the manufacture of a product. An example of this is the expensive safety and pollution-control equipment mandated for new cars, an added production cost that cuts into the profitability of auto manufacturers.

International diversification of risks is an important motivation for foreign investment. Companies also invest in foreign countries to counter the investment actions of competitors. For example, if a manufacturing company establishes a factory in a foreign country, a competitor is likely to make a similar investment in the same country.

The financial manager of a multinational corporation (MNC) should analyze the assets and the earnings derived in each foreign country. Useful ratios are:

• Questionable foreign revenue to total revenue.
• Questionable foreign earnings to net income.
• Total export revenue to total revenue.
• Total export earnings to net income.
• Total assets in questionable or politically unstable foreign countries to total assets.

Many MNCs and banks attempt to measure the political risks they face. They even hire or employ political risk analysts. Several independent services provide political risk and country risk ratings, including:

• *Country Risk Rating*, put out annually by *Euromoney* magazine, is based on a country's access to international credit, trade finance, political risk, and payment record. The rankings are generally confirmed by political risk insurers and top syndicate managers in the Euromarkets.

• *Economist Intelligence Unit Rating*, by a New York-based subsidiary of the London Economist Group, is based on such factors as external debt and trends in the current account, consistency of government policy, foreign-exchange reserves, and the quality of economic management.

• *International Country Risk Guide* is a rating is put out by a U.S. division of International Business Communications, Ltd., London. It offers a composite risk rating, as well as individual ratings for political, financial, and economic risk. The political variable— which makes up half the composite index—includes factors such as government corruption and how economic expectations diverge from reality. The financial rating looks at such things as the likelihood of losses from exchange controls and loan defaults. Finally, economic ratings consider such factors as inflation and debt-service costs.

Another area to be analyzed for political risk is government contracts. Determine the percentage of earnings derived from government contract work and subsidies and the degree to which such work and subsidies are recurring.

Also determine the current and prospective effects on the company of government interference by reviewing current and proposed laws and regulations as indicated in legislative hearings, trade journals, and newspapers.

REPAIR

- Investigate the current political status of each country where the company operates.
- Establish a joint venture with a local entrepreneur.
- Buy insurance when political risk in a foreign country is high. In the U.S., the Eximbank offers policies to exporters that cover such political risks as war, currency inconvertibility, and civil unrest. The Overseas Private Investment Corporation (OPIC) offers policies to U.S. investors abroad to cover such risks as currency inconvertibility, civil or foreign war damages, or expropriation. Similar policies are offered in the U.K. by the Export Credit Guarantee Department (ECGD), in Canada by the Export Development Council (EDC), and in Germany by an agency called Hermes.
- Engage in forward exchange contracts to minimize exchange risk.
- Diversify across countries.
- Diversify into activities that are not overly dependent on government business if current operations are overly reliant on government contracts and subsidies.
- Lobby to keep legislators favorably disposed toward the company.

PREVENTION TECHNIQUES

- Evaluate the risk/return trade-off.
- Understand foreign customs and laws before starting operations abroad.
- Hire consultants in the country where operations are to be located to assess the current political climate and make contact with important officials to prevent any unforeseen political or operating problems.
- Establish a department (a mini-State Department) to assess foreign political developments that may affect the company.
- Familiarize yourself with the domestic, local, and foreign regulatory environments in which the company and its subsidiaries operate.
- Use foreign brokers when specialized knowledge is needed.
- Promote a good relationship with regulatory agencies.
- Establish a public relations program to counteract proposed legislation that might adversely affect company earnings.
- Plan carefully to minimize taxes. Study foreign tax treaties to determine whether they contain provisions your company can use to its advantage.
- Determine which foreign countries offer tax incentives to foreign companies establishing operations within their borders.

SPILLOVER EFFECTS

- Lower earning power and cash flow.
- Negative impact on the market price of stock and bonds.
- Costly legal actions.
- Adverse publicity.
- Operating conditions so negative that the company is forced out of a country.

See also in this chapter: RISK DISPROPORTIONATE TO RETURN *and* RISK IN CORPORATE OPERATIONS.

PROBLEM
FOREIGN EXCHANGE RISK

SYMPTOM

Exchange rates for dealing in foreign currencies are moving in unexpected directions.

CAUSE

Companies operating abroad are exposed to foreign exchange risk, particularly in countries having significant fluctuation in exchange rates.

ANALYSIS

The globalization of the world economy and the devaluation of the U. S. dollar have allowed many American companies to enter foreign markets. A company may be exposed to foreign exchange risk whenever it participates in international markets. Sales revenues may be collected in one currency, assets denominated in another, and profits measured in a third. Changes in exchange rates can adversely affect sales by making competing imported goods cheaper.

Speculative foreign currency exposure is due to risk-prone financial management. Exposure to losses on purchase or sales commitments can result from the foreign exchange contracts themselves.

Look at how the company is exposed in each foreign country where it has a major operation. The degree of fluctuation of the foreign exchange rate may be measured by its percentage change over time or by its standard deviation (or both). Examine the trends in the ratio of foreign exchange gains and losses to net income and to total revenue, and look at the trend in losses on purchase and sales contracts over time.

REPAIR

Forecast foreign exchange risks by considering:
• Recent rate movements.
• Foreign inflation rates.
• Balance of payments and trade.
• Money supply growth.
• Interest rate differentials.
• Adopt a conservative foreign exchange posture.
• Bill customers in the currency in which the company reports.

- Buy and sell forward exchange contracts in foreign currencies.
- Diversify and finance internationally.

PREVENTION TECHNIQUES

- Minimize transaction exposure by:
  - —Executing contracts in the forward exchange market or in the foreign exchange futures.
  - —Borrowing U.S. funds and investing them in securities of the country where the foreign credit purchase was made.
- Balance foreign assets and liabilities to protect the company from exchange rate fluctuations and profit variability.
- Operate only in countries having stable rates.
- Establish a foreign asset management program that uses such strategies as switching cash and other currencies into strong currencies while piling up debt and other liabilities in depreciating currencies.
- Offer discounts to encourage quick collection in weak currencies.
- Offer liberal credit terms to customers paying in strong currencies.

SPILLOVER EFFECTS

- Excessive brokerage fees for executing foreign exchange contracts.
- Decline in profitability and cash flow.
- Investor uncertainty.
- Accounting and tax problems.

PROBLEM
SOCIAL AND ENVIRONMENTAL RISKS
SYMPTOMS

- Customers and the general public have a negative image of the business.
- Environmental conditions cause operating losses and shutdowns.
- The company causes pollution or creates hazardous waste.

CAUSES

Social risk may be caused by:

- Strained ethnic, religious, sexual, age, and political conflicts.
- Adverse or atypical weather conditions (particularly in the case of recreational businesses like resorts).
- An absence or breakdown of pollution control equipment, bringing on government intervention and fines.

ANALYSIS

Business enterprises have traditionally sought to maximize short-term profits while observing the minimal environmental protection required by law. Disregard of the environment by large corporations has now become a matter of public concern. Ask:

- Does the company have a reputation for employee discrimination?
- Is the company perceived as callous about public issues or the environment?
- Is worker safety of paramount importance?
- Has the federal government found violations of the Occupational Safety and Health Act (OSHA)?
- Does the company have a fair health insurance coverage plan for its workers?
- Is business affected by the idiosyncrasies of nature?

REPAIR

- Improve the company's image by putting more time and money into public relations.
- Hire local residents.
- Hire and promote qualified minorities and women.
- Contribute to welfare and civic improvement programs.
- Sell marginally profitable operations that are the target of government regulation and environmental groups.
- Make worker safety a major company policy.
- Determine whether employee medical coverage is adequate.

PREVENTIVE TECHNIQUES

- Strictly enforce product quality guidelines.
- Advertise in local newspapers to explain the company's support of community activities.
- Sponsor training workshops in low-employment areas and hire qualified people who successfully complete the course.
- Settle discrimination eases out of court.
- Install new pollution-control equipment and upgrade what you already have.
- Reevaluate the company's geographic location.

SPILLOVER EFFECTS

- Declining earning power.
- Increased costs.
- Lawsuits.
- Fines.

PROBLEM
MANAGEMENT UNAWARE OF FINANCIAL PROBLEMS

SYMPTOMS

- Costly inventory buildups.
- Excessive production costs.
- Operating inefficiencies.
- Uncoordinated and incompatible programs.

CAUSES

- Failure to consult with on-the-job personnel.
- Failure to issue current, clear, and concise directives.
- Issuing too many memoranda.
- Upper management belief that it can solve all financial and operating problems by itself.

ANALYSIS

Communication of data is fundamental to controlling operations and reducing uncertainty and losses in any organization. Communication is essential to ensure that employees carry out their functions, thereby enabling the organization to meet its production goals, generate new ideas, and foster employee self-esteem and morale. The company should study the adverse financial effects of poor communication on company policy, major acquisitions or divestitures, or operating segments of the business.

REPAIR

- Have top management consult regularly with operating managers before making most decisions.
- Encourage top management to use a variety of techniques for transmitting information downward in the organization:
  - Bulletin boards.
  - Regular meetings of upper managers, supervisors, and employees.
  - Company publications.
  - Payroll inserts.
- Encourage communication by lower managers:
  - Informal discussions with employees.
  - Exit interviews.
  - Discussions with union officials.
  - Review of union grievances.
  - Cash bonuses for valuable employee suggestions.
  - Communication sessions in which employees are encouraged to fire questions at executives about the operations of the business.

PREVENTION TECHNIQUES

- Make communications as clear and concise as possible.
- Ensure that there is straightforward and honest interaction among different levels of management.
- Review potential company actions in light of their impact on employees.
- Form a policy committee to set and oversee an effective communications policy.

SPILLOVER EFFECTS

Failure to adequately plan operating policy may result in:
- Declining profitability.
- Cost inefficiencies.
- Operating bottlenecks.
- Possible bankruptcy.

Chapter 9

Budgeting and Forecasting Problems

If actual costs exceed expected costs, profits fall. If actual revenue is less than expected revenue, the fault may lie in either product quality or sales effort, or both.

Differences between actual and budgeted costs signal inefficiencies that require immediate corrective action. Often, the problem is poor financial planning, reflected in erroneous or unrealistic budget figures. If sales and expense estimates are not reasonable, the entire planning and control process must be questioned.

A company will miss the mark if it does not have the right product at the most opportune time. Poor use of manufacturing facilities can cause scheduling problems and cost overruns. And, of course, without adequate financial resources, the company cannot grow.

This chapter covers the following financial problems:

• Actual costs exceeding budgeted costs.
• Actual costs exceeding standard costs.
• Actual revenue below standard revenue.
• Inaccurate sales and expense estimates.
• Lack of the right product at the right time.
• Poor use of production capacity.
• Expansion outfacing financial resources.

PROBLEM
ACTUAL COSTS EXCEEDING
BUDGETED COSTS

SYMPTOMS

- Lack of funds available toward the end of the accounting period.
- Consistently too-tight budget estimates that no one can realistically meet.
- Significant differences between budgeted and actual expenditures.

CAUSES

- Inexperienced management.
- Lack of cost control and planning.
- Lack of efficiency in cost management.
- Experimental ("pet") projects that do not meet the company's profit goals.
- Duplication of effort and facilities.
- Waste.
- Budgets based on historical experience rather than the current operating environment.
- Use of a static (fixed) budget geared for only one level of activity.

ANALYSIS

The variance between budgeted and actual costs for each major product line item should be examined over a full operating period to determine who is responsible for the deviation and why, and to take corrective steps.

Flexible budgeting differentiates between fixed and variable costs, thus allowing for a budget that can be automatically adjusted through changes in variable-cost totals to the level of activity actually attained. Thus, variances between actual and budgeted costs should be adjusted for volume variations before differences due to price and quantity factors are computed.

The flexible budget, unlike the static budget, can help provide accurate measurements of performance by comparing actual costs for a given output with budgeted costs for the same level of output. A flexible budget is geared toward a range of activity rather than a single level of activity, and it is dynamic. A series of budgets can be drawn up for various activity levels.

REPAIR

- Implement a program to trim excessive expenditure.
- Restructure and reorganize to make the company leaner and more efficient.
- Eliminate duplicate activities and facilities.
- Merge operations to generate cost efficiencies.
- Consolidate facilities and equipment to achieve more efficient production.
- Subcontract out some work if it can be done at a lower cost.
- Obtain union concessions to reduce wages and fringe benefits or to increase productivity.
- Evaluate leased premises to reduce rental charges. (Closely examine square footage prices, commercial rent tax, and escalation clauses.)
- Cut back on travel costs by using conference calls and video teleconferences.
- Enter into joint ventures to cut costs and eliminate duplications.
- Implement an energy-conservation program.
- Identify variances early in the evaluation process.
- If variances are due to poor estimation, redesign the budgeting process.
- Obtain more favorable credit terms from suppliers.

PREVENTION TECHNIQUES

- Formulate a cost-control program.
- Place caps on expense categories (such as travel and entertainment) and require special permission to exceed the maximums.
- Reduce advertising and promotional expense, if that can be done without jeopardizing sales.
- Assign each employee an identification number for copy machine, fax, and computer use to prevent abuse.
- Undertake an engineering study to see if manufactured items can be redesigned to save costs.

- Use financial models to make sure all relevant variances are included in budgets.
- Use a flexible budget.

SPILLOVER EFFECTS

- If costs are not controlled, earnings will fall off significantly.
- Business operations will be deficient and productivity will be adversely affected.
- Future planning will be inaccurate.

See also in this chapter ACTUAL COSTS EXCEEDING STANDARD COSTS. *In Chapter 6*: INADEQUATE COST CONTROLS.

PROBLEM
ACTUAL COSTS EXCEEDING STANDARD COSTS

SYMPTOMS

- Excess costs.
- Manufacturing delays.
- Inefficient budgeting.
- Waste.
- Idle production facilities.
- A wide difference between production and sales.
- Inferior quality of manufactured goods.

CAUSES

- Actual costs exceed standard costs because managers are ineffective.
- Standards are out-of-date or inaccurate because of poor budget estimates.
- Price (rate, spending) variances are unfavorable due to material price increases, labor rate increases, and inadequate cost control.
- Quantity (usage) variances are unfavorable due to poor quality of raw materials, lack of supervision, or incompetent workers.
- Production volume is consistently unfavorable for any of a number of reasons, among them inadequate facilities, inefficient scheduling, lack of orders, defective raw materials, incorrect tool-

ing, lack of employee productivity, machine breakdowns, long operating times, and failure to obtain raw materials on time.

ANALYSIS

A standard cost is the estimated cost of manufacturing an item during a given future production period. An unfavorable cost variance indicates that actual costs exceed standard costs. Variances can be arrived at only when the actual figures are known at the end of the production period. When a product is produced or a service is performed, the following three items must be determined:

1. *Actual cost*. This equals actual price times actual quantity. Actual quantity equals actual quantity per unit of work times actual units of work produced.
2. *Standard cost*. This equals standard price times standard quantity. Standard quantity equals standard quantity per unit of work times actual units of work produced.
3. *Total (control) variance*. This equals actual cost less standard cost. Total variance has the following elements:

Price (rate, spending) variance
= (Standard price - Actual price) x Actual quantity.
Quantity (usage, efficiency) variance
= (Standard quantity - Actual quantity) Standard price.

These are computed for both material and labor. A variance is unfavorable when actual cost is higher than standard cost.

REPAIR

• Improve the budgeting process.
• Institute a cost-reduction program.
• Pinpoint the party or parties responsible.
• To correct an unfavorable material price variance, increase the selling price of the goods produced, substitute cheaper materials, change a production method or specification, engage in a cost-reduction program, and combine resources.
• To correct unfavorable labor efficiency, buy better machinery, revise plant layout, improve operating methods, and upgrade employee training and development.

- Improve a volume variance through better scheduling and supervision.
- Make volume purchases when discounts are attractive.
- Perform inspection at key points in the manufacturing cycle.

PREVENTION TECHNIQUES

- Standards should be modified when they no longer reflect current conditions.
- Use the management-by-exception principle to highlight problem areas.
- Computerize variance reporting for immediate feedback and analysis.
- Adjust output levels.
- Evaluate the purchasing department to assure that it is obtaining the best possible material at the lowest possible price.
- Consider vertical integration to reduce the price and supply risk of raw materials.
- Institute a regular maintenance schedule to improve the functioning of machinery.
- Improve employees' knowledge and efficiency.

SPILLOVER EFFECTS

Lack of cost control will result in an item at a higher cost that does not meet standards. Unfavorable cost variances (and the resultant higher selling prices) will lead to less competitiveness in the marketplace and less profitability. Unless costs are controllable in the future, the business may fail.

See also in this chapter: ACTUAL COSTS EXCEEDING BUDGETED COSTS. *In Chapter 6:* INADEQUATE COST CONTROLS.

PROBLEM
ACTUAL REVENUE BELOW STANDARD REVENUE

SYMPTOMS

- Reduced selling price.
- Decline in sales volume and market share.

- Increase in sales returns.
- Ineffective advertising.

CAUSES

- Sales price variance is unfavorable because the product is being sold at a discount.
- Sales volume variance is unfavorable because of an inaccurate standard, poor sales effort, and loss of market position.
- Sales are unfavorable because of poor quality.

ANALYSIS

The total sales variance equals expected sales revenue less actual sales revenue. It should be separated into price and volume and then each should be analyzed for the reasons behind the variance:

Sales price variance
= (Actual selling price - Budgeted selling price) x Actual units sold.

Sales volume variance
= (Actual quantity - Budgeted quantity) x Budgeted selling price.

The sales variances are computed to gauge the performance of the marketing function. Examine the variances by salesperson to determine the effectiveness of the sales force in terms of cost and time spent. Salesperson variances are determined as follows:

Total cost variance = Actual cost - Standard cost.
Variance in salesperson days
= (Actual days - Standard days) x Standard rate per day.
Variance in salesperson costs
= (Actual rate - Standard rate) x Actual days.
Total variance in calls =
(Actual calls - Actual sale) versus (Standard calls - Standard sale).
Variance in calls = (Actual calls - Standard calls) x Standard sale.
Variance in sales = (Actual sale - Standard sale) x Standard calls.
Joint variance
= (Actual calls - Standard calls) x (Actual sale - Standard sale).

REPAIR

- Improve sales planning and forecasting.
- If necessary, improve product quality, design, packaging, or sales mix.
- Dispose of outdated styles and slow-moving stock.
- Identify who is responsible for sales variances and take corrective action.
- Increase prices, if the market will bear it.
- To stimulate sales, offer better services, launch as many new products as possible, offer sales promotions, provide rebates, offer discounts, and give zero percent financing.

PREVENTION TECHNIQUES

- If the total sales variance is unfavorable, concentrate on the marketing aspects, because the variance indicates a problem with sales, advertising, and pricing.
- Use a computerized spreadsheets program to determine sales variances by product.
- Track salesperson costs against budgeted figures.
- Pay higher commission rates to salespeople on high-profit-margin items and slow-moving ones.

SPILLOVER EFFECTS

If revenue is less than expected, the business will be less profitable than anticipated. A decline in the revenue base may cause layoffs and other cost-cutting measures. The survival of a business is questionable if sales continue to slide.

PROBLEM
INACCURATE SALES AND
EXPENSE ESTIMATES

SYMPTOM

Actual expenditures are substantially different from what was projected.

CAUSES

- Computational errors.
- Incorrect application of budgetary procedures.

- Incorrect forecasting of variables to which specific revenues or expenditures are related.
- Failure to anticipate unusual occurrences (e.g., an uninsured catastrophe).
- Intentional overestimating of projected expenditures to enhance the appearance of superior performance.
- Intentional overestimating of revenues to satisfy current and potential investors and creditors.
- Failure to consult with the managers of specific performance centers.
- Failure to use sophisticated forecasting models that incorporate all explanatory variables.
- Lack of careful planning.

ANALYSIS

Actual revenues and expenses should be compared to estimated revenues and expenses. If significant differences exist over time, the budgetary process is deficient. The reasons for the discrepancies should be analyzed and corrective action taken.

REPAIR

- Analyze how budgets are prepared.
- Compare budgeted to actual figures.
- Include departmental and sales managers in the process.
- Use experienced staff and budgeting software to prevent mathematical errors.

PREVENTION TECHNIQUES

- Improve forecasting procedures.
- Include marketing and production managers, financial planners, and accountants in the planning process.
- Use forecasts that take into account the economic environment in which the business operates.
- Use financial planning models to take into account all the variables that can affect the estimates.

SPILLOVER EFFECTS

- Deficient budgeting reflects a managerial lack of careful planning, control, and direction.

- Inaccurate predictions of future revenue and expenses mean that planning is inefficient. The resulting baseless decision-making can negatively affect company performance, growth, and profitability.
- Inaccurate sales projections result in inaccurate production estimates and the hiring of either too many or too few employees.
- If sales estimates are off, the expected production volume will also be incorrect, which can lead to excessive buildup in inventory and exposure to possible future inventory write-offs because of obsolescence.
- Manufacturing costs will be exceptionally high and unproductive.

See also in this chapter: ACTUAL COSTS EXCEEDING BUDGETED COSTS.

PROBLEM
LACK OF THE RIGHT PRODUCT
AT THE RIGHT TIME

SYMPTOMS

- New products failing because of lack of customer demand.
- Products introduced at the wrong times.

CAUSES

- Heavy competition.
- Poor marketing.
- Insufficient planning.
- Inadequate production budget.
- Poor product design.

ANALYSIS

- Compute the ratio of failed products to total products.
- Determine why a product failed, what losses have occurred, and who was responsible.
- Analyze the product's research and development costs.

REPAIR

- Advertise more to improve customer awareness and demand.
- Strengthen sales efforts.

PREVENTION TECHNIQUES

- Market analysis of consumer demands.
- Product planning and analysis.
- Cost feasibility studies.

SPILLOVER EFFECTS

- The business will lose money.
- The company's growth rate will decline.
- Customers will lose faith in the company's products.
- The reputation of the business will suffer.

PROBLEM
POOR USE OF PRODUCTION CAPACITY

SYMPTOMS

- Increasing expenditures on manufacturing.
- Downtime.
- Failure to meet production schedules.
- Poor-quality manufactured goods.
- Increased repair costs.

CAUSES

- Poor production planning and analysis.
- Poor supervision, design, and scheduling by engineers.
- Obsolete and malfunctioning equipment.
- Failure to test operations randomly.
- Inexperienced or incompetent workers.
- Purchase of the wrong equipment.
- Failure to use quantitative techniques such as linear programming (allocation of limited resources to maximize gain and minimize cost).

ANALYSIS

Measures that may be used to evaluate the efficiency productive capacity are:

- Number and length of machine breakdowns.
- Output per employee-hour.
- Input-output relationship (what was put in, in terms of time and money, versus what was put out, in terms of quantity and quality).
- The trend in the ratio of manufacturing costs to total costs and to revenue.
- The trend in the ratio of indirect to direct labor hours.
- The trend in the ratio of repairs and maintenance to the carrying value of equipment.
- The number and duration of manufacturing delays.
- Order backlogs.
- Variances between budgeted and actual production volume and costs.

The ratio of indirect to direct labor monitors indirect manpower planning and control. A declining trend is unfavorable because it indicates that management has not maintained a desirable relationship between indirect and direct personnel.

A decline in the operating assets ratio (operating to total assets) means operations and production capacity are worsening. The operating ratio concentrates on those assets actively employed in current operations, not those that are past-oriented or future-oriented. Past-oriented assets are not, strictly speaking, assets at all. They are the result of prior errors, inefficiencies, or losses because of competitive factors or changes in business plans but have not yet been formally recognized in the accounts by being written off. Examples are obsolete goods, idle plants, receivables under litigation, delinquent receivables, and nonperforming loans (no interest being recognized). Future-oriented assets are acquired for corporate growth or generating future sales. Examples are land held for speculation and factories under construction. Nonoperating assets reduce profits and return on investment because they offer no benefit to current operations. They neither generate sales nor reduce costs. They are a drain on the company.

The ratios of sales dollars or sales volume to the number of employees or to salaries are an indicator of employee productivity. Low ratios mean that employee time spent and payroll incurred are not being used productively.

REPAIR

- Track down and replace those responsible for poor use of manufacturing facilities.
- Subcontract work.
- Increase inspection at key points in the manufacturing process.
- Keep productive assets well maintained and replace obsolete fixed assets.
- Improve employee training and morale.

PREVENTION TECHNIQUES

- Replace obsolete and ineffective machinery.
- Improve training and instruction in machine use.
- Improve coordination among all parties to manufacturing.

SPILLOVER EFFECTS

- Increased operating costs.
- Lower profits.
- Manufacturing delays.
- Machinery breakdowns.

See in Chapter 4: EXCESSIVE COST IN RELATION TO PRODUCTION VOLUME.

PROBLEM
EXPANSION OUTPACING FINANCIAL RESOURCES

SYMPTOMS

- No funds are available for sustained capital growth.
- Capital expenditures must be reduced because of the delay in receiving debt and equity funds.

CAUSES

- A shortage in the money supply.
- Poor economic conditions.
- Deficient corporate financial health.
- Industry problems.
- Growth that outstrips the company's financial resources.
- Lower credit rating.
- Risky projects undertaken with inadequate cash resources.

ANALYSIS

Evaluate the trend in the ratio of capital expansion to dollar financing obtained. A high ratio may mean that investment in property, plant, and equipment is not adequately supported by outside funds. Restrictions on the use of funds by lenders may indicate apprehension about the company's capital investments. The ratio of debt to assets will also indicate the amount of debt incurred to obtain assets.

REPAIR

- Cut back on expansion or obtain additional financing.
- Enter into joint ventures to diversify financial backing.

PREVENTION TECHNIQUES

- Improve planning for the acquisition of capital facilities.
- Reduce expansion efforts.
- Secure new lines of credit.
- Synchronize cash outlays to cash inflows.
- Undertake joint ventures with other enterprises.
- More accurately forecast the demand for capital expenditures.

SPILLOVER EFFECTS

If the business expands without adequate financial support, it may be unable to complete its proposed projects, turning them into nonproductive assets that tie up corporate resources without adequate return. That situation that will erode profitability or cause operating losses.

Chapter 10
Noncompetitive Compensation

Financial problems result when employees are overcompensated in salaries and fringe benefits, including pension and health care. Compensation should be tied to productivity. A business cannot stay afloat if its labor costs are more than the value of its employee output. On the other hand, it cannot keep good employees if they are not properly compensated.

An obvious indication of danger is that employee labor hours and costs are increasing while production volume is decreasing. A declining trend in revenue per employee (sales divided by number of employees) is another ominous sign. Management must immediately correct any quality problems in manufactured goods due to inferior workmanship but should also examine employee turnover, absences, and slowdowns.

In this chapter, we evaluate the following problems:

• Low financial incentive for employee productivity.

• Unfunded retirement benefits.

PROBLEM
LOW FINANCIAL INCENTIVE FOR EMPLOYEE PRODUCTIVITY

SYMPTOMS

• High absenteeism and turnover.
• Escalating incentive costs but no reduction in employee absenteeism and turnover.

CAUSES

• Low pay.
• Inadequate or nonexistent fringe benefit package.

ANALYSIS

Effective compensation is essential to employee satisfaction. The compensation should be adequate, equitable, balanced, and cost-effective. It should provide both an incentive for satisfactory job performance and a reward for productive work. The fringe benefits package might include stock option and bonus plans, pension and profit-sharing plans, group life insurance, hospitalization and medical plans, and death payments. Despite the escalating costs of fringe benefits, management has no choice but to offer at least some.

REPAIR

• Draw up a compensation and incentive budget.
• Try to create plans that employees want.
• Hire a compensation and incentive benefits expert.
• After comparing your own compensation and fringe benefits costs to those of other firms with the aid of data from an industry or professional group or sources like the Chamber of Commerce, try to at least match their plans.
• Provide for no-cost or low-cost benefits. For example, airlines provide discount stand-by tickets to employees and their families.
• Offer a deferred-compensation plan so that employees can defer compensation and related taxes until retirement.

PREVENTION TECHNIQUES

- Set objectives for the compensation strategy.
- Involve participants and unions in the benefits program.
- Explain the benefits package to employees thoroughly.
- Monitor all financial costs.
- Encourage employees to help decide what benefits they should be offered.

SPILLOVER EFFECTS

Lack of adequate compensation for employee productivity will result in morale problems, less employee cooperation, decreased productivity, strikes, and turnover.

PROBLEM
UNFUNDED RETIREMENT BENEFITS

SYMPTOMS

- Cash flow problems.
- Failure to meet funding requirements.
- Failure to make fund contributions.

CAUSES

- Poor management.
- Extravagant funding requirements.
- Over-generous ancillary benefits.
- Erroneous actuarial assumptions.

ANALYSIS

Virtually all qualified retirement plans entail significant costs to the employer. Pension plans, including defined benefit and money purchase plans, require a certain level of annual funding. Contributions are made periodically to a trustee or insurance company that invests the funds until employees are entitled to receive distributions. The amount and timing of the contribution is determined by the specific type of plan. Certain plans must also pay insurance premiums to the Pension Benefit Guaranty Corporation (PBGC), a government agency that ensures that benefits will be available to retirees even if the employer-funded trust is insufficient.

REPAIR

- Use outside auditors to review monthly the adequacy of the amounts funded.
- Hire a pension trustee who will report any discrepancies or deviation from fund requirements to top management.
- Hire an actuary to determine whether the assumptions used to fund the plan were computed correctly.
- Try to amend the plan.
- Reduce ancillary benefits.
- Restrict bonuses and commissions.
- Seek to extend the time for filing the company's tax return. This extension will also serve as an extension for making a contribution to the pension plan. For example, a calendar-year employer with a pension plan can, for 20X2, make a contribution by September 15, 20X3, and avoid a funding deficiency.
- Pay administrative expenses from plan assets.
- Make contributions in property other than cash.
- Terminate overfunded defined benefit plans.
- Cut total payroll costs by reducing the workforce.
- Set up plans that can be funded exclusively with employee salary deferrals without employer contributions.

PREVENTION TECHNIQUES

- Continual audit by outside auditors to prevent unauthorized use of pension funds.
- A pension committee chosen from among the corporate directors (or the partners if the company a partnership) to oversee operation and funding of the pension plan.
- An investment manager who can acquire, manage, and dispose of plan assets.

SPILLOVER EFFECTS

An employer who fails to meet funding obligations requirements may incur liabilities to the retirement plan, the IRS, the PBGC, and the Department of Labor. The employer may be sued by a plan participant to enforce its obligation to make the required employer contribution.

According to new rules of the Financial Accounting Standards Board, a company must now record costs associated with postretirement health care benefits in the years in which employee services are performed. Many companies have made inadequate provisions on their books. As a result, huge expenses and liabilities may have to be recorded, with significantly adverse effects on reported net income and balance-sheet position. There is likely to be a drastic decline in earnings from the charge-off, reduced cash flow from making up for previous underfunding of the plan, and recognition of increased debt.

See in Chapter 6: EXCESSIVE LABOR COSTS.

Chapter 11

Sales and Advertising Miss Margins

A business has a serious financial problem when its sales base is eroding. Advertising is not effective when it does not generate sales dollars.

The problems can become acute when a lowered selling price actually shrinks profit margins because of rising costs. A high level of product returns means customer dissatisfaction and a loss in current and future business. A business cannot survive for long with a negative reputation Management must also rethink its policy of increasing product or service pricing when either one causes sales to fall off.

The following financial problems are considered in this chapter:
- Unprofitable advertising expenditures.
- Revenue base erosion.
- Sales reduced by higher prices.
- Margins shrunk by lower prices.
- Increasing merchandise returns.

PROBLEM
UNPROFITABLE ADVERTISING EXPENDITURES

SYMPTOM

Advertising expenditures are increasing but sales are flat or declining.

CAUSES

- Poor planning by the marketing department.
- Poor economic conditions making consumers reluctant to spend.
- Inaccurate or incompetent advertising.

ANALYSIS

Advertising effectiveness should be measured and controlled. A comparison should be made over time using the ratios of advertising to sales and advertising to net income. A higher ratio may indicate that the advertising is ineffective because advertising costs are being incurred without a significant impact on sales volume.

- Look at sales and profit before, during, and after an advertising campaign. If a campaign does not increase sales, it is a failure.
- Do media surveys to determine whether your advertising is reaching your target audience in sufficient numbers.
- Determine whether advertising dollars are being spent in accordance with established company policy.
- Analyze trends in company advertising over time relative to those of competing companies within the industry.

REPAIR

- Analyze why an advertising campaign is not working and then eliminate or improve it.
- If sales are down because of high pricing, reduce the selling price.

PREVENTION TECHNIQUES

- Undertake a thorough marketing study to find the best way of advertising to reach the targeted audience.
- Do a cost/benefit analysis before the advertising campaign begins to assure that the campaign is worth the expense.

- Carefully appraise what the competition is doing.

SPILLOVER EFFECTS

If advertising expenditures do not generate sufficient revenue, the excessive costs will lower profitability.

PROBLEM
REVENUE BASE EROSION

SYMPTOMS

- A decline in sales and other sources of revenue.
- A loss in market share.
- Selling prices marked down.
- Products reaching the final stage of their cycle (down stage).
- Patented new products failing to appear.
- Lack of customer demand, interest, and confidence.
- Loss of a major customer.
- A deteriorating reputation.

CAUSES

- Poor economic environment.
- Poor product mix.
- A saturated market because of oversupply, competition, or technological obsolescence.
- No new opportunities.
- A high-risk product line.
- Disappearing export sales.

ANALYSIS

- Compute the trends over the last 10 years in (1) sales and nonoperating income sources, (2) the ratio of sales to net income, and (3) the ratio of nonoperating income to net income. Declining ratios are cause for concern.
- Determine the trend in the company's replacement and maintenance expense revenue as a percentage of (1) new sales, (2) total revenue, and (3) net income. Increasing trends indicate eroding revenue.

- Calculate the percentage of nonoperating income to total revenue and net income. A high ratio indicates a coming decline in revenue.
- Determine the variability in volume, price, and cost of each major product.
- Calculate the revenue derived from growth, mature, declining, and developmental products. A high percentage deriving from declining and developmental products is a negative sign.
- Analyze the sales backlog to monitor sales status and planning.

REPAIR

- Diversify the product line and customer base.
- Expand abroad.
- Design products whose sales will generate further sources of revenue. (An example is Xerox, which provides maintenance services and replacement parts to its customers.)
- Reduce risk in the product line.
- Establish joint ventures with foreign companies to enter overseas markets.

PREVENTION TECHNIQUES

- Keep current with the latest technological developments.
- Engage in long-term contracts to assure steady business.
- Enter countercyclical lines of business to insulate the company against economic cycles.
- Manufacture or buy products whose cost and price are stable.
- Introduce new products regularly to replace ones that are losing their market appeal.
- Acquire competitors to gain more control of market conditions.
- Develop a product line of low-priced goods that can substitute for higher-priced goods as a built-in hedge against inflation and recession.
- Develop a piggyback product base (similar products associated with the company's prime product or base business).

SPILLOVER EFFECTS

An eroding revenue base will negatively affect future sales and profitability. The business may experience serious liquidity problems because lackluster performance lowers cash inflow.

See in Chapter 4: LOSS RESULTING FROM PRODUCT REFINEMENT *and* WEAK SALES MIX. *In Chapter 9:* ACTUAL REVENUE BELOW STANDARD REVENUE.

PROBLEM
SALES REDUCED BY HIGHER PRICES

SYMPTOMS

- Customers shift to lower-priced items in the product line or to a competitor's product.
- Customers complain about the higher price.

CAUSES

- A recession causes consumers to watch their spending.
- Customers are reluctant to pay more for a familiar product.

ANALYSIS

A reduction in sales volume when the selling price is increased means that demand for the product may be elastic. Determine the elasticity of the product to see the effect on volume as selling price is changed (*see* LACK OF DIVERSIFICATION *in Chapter 8* for an illustration of this computation).

Determine the effect on profit at different selling prices by using a "what-if" analysis using a spreadsheet computer program. Which selling price maximizes profit?

Assuming capacity is idled, as is typically the case, total fixed cost remains the same with declining sales volume, resulting in an increase in fixed cost per unit. While total variable costs will decline as production decreases, variable cost per unit will be the same.

REPAIR

- Establish an appropriate price for a product or service based on costs, desired markup, capacity, supply/demand relationship, and competitive factors.
- Test selling at a lower price to se how that affects volume.
- Attempt to move toward products with inelastic demand where a change in selling price will not affect volume.
- Promote the quality and reliability of the company's products and services.
- Try marketing a substitute product that can be sold for less.

PREVENTION TECHNIQUES

- Redesign the product to reduce manufacturing costs so that it can be sold at the same price.
- Try to reduce material, labor, and overhead costs, so that prices don't have to be increased (or increased any further).
- Test-market the product at different selling prices to see which price consumers find more attractive.
- Use a simulation ("what-if") model to estimate the effects of alternative selling price changes on sales volume.

SPILLOVER EFFECTS

- The profitability of the business may remain flat or even decline.
- Customer loyalty to the company's other products may diminish.
- The company's market share and ability to maintain future operations may decline.

See in Chapter 6: PRICING THAT LOWERS PROFITS.

PROBLEM
MARGINS SHRUNK BY LOWERED PRICES

Symptoms
- The reduced prices reduce the firm's profit margin (net income/sales).
- The reduced prices increase sales volume, but the profit margin on each item sold is less.

CAUSES

It may be necessary to lower prices to:
- Perk up sluggish consumer demand, particularly in recessionary times.
- Reduce a buildup in inventory of slow-moving items.
- Encourage customers to buy more items in the product line.
- Attract new customers.
- Retain old customers.

ANALYSIS

A business should accept an order at below-normal price when:
- Idle capacity exists (since fixed cost remains constant), as long as there is a *contribution margin* on the order. (The contribution margin equals price less variable costs.)
- The company is in financial distress.
- It is in a competitive bidding situation.

Example: Currently, 10,000 units are sold at $30 per unit. Variable cost per unit is $18 and fixed costs total $100,000, so fixed cost per unit is $10 ($100,000/10,000). There is idle capacity. A prospective customer wants to buy 100 units at only $20 per unit.

Ignoring other market considerations (for example, unfavorable reaction by customers paying $30 per unit), you should recommend the sale of the additional 100 units. Why? Because it results in a positive additional (marginal) profit of $200, as shown in Table 11.1.

REPAIR

- Reduce variable costs to maintain the same profit margin.
- Reduce manufacturing costs through redesign, cutting quality, reducing size, and so on.
- Reduce discretionary fixed costs (e.g., advertising, research and development).

PREVENTION TECHNIQUES

Use contribution margin analysis to determine when the selling price can be lowered without eliminating incremental profitability. The rule of thumb is to accept an order below the normal price as long as there is a contribution margin to cover total fixed costs.

TABLE 11.1. CALCULATING CONTRIBUTION MARGIN

Sales (100 x $20)	$2,000
Less variable cost (100 x $18)	(1,800)
Contribution margin	$200
Less fixed cost	0*
Net income	$ 200

*Because of idle capacity, there is no additional fixed cost. If the order were to increase fixed cost by $50, say, because it required a special tool, it is still financially advantageous to sell the item at $20. The additional profit is now $150, as illustrated in the next instance.

Sales (100 x $20)	$2000
Less variable cost (100 x $18)	(1,800)
Contribution margin	$200
Less fixed cost	(50)
Net income	$150

SPILLOVER EFFECTS

Reducing the selling price leads to a lower profit per sales dollar. Customers who bought at the higher price may resent the price reduction. Therefore, the business should try to minimize the pain by referring to what happened as, say, a discount sale, rebate, or closeout.

See in Chapter 6: PRICING THAT LOWERS PROFITS

PROBLEM
INCREASING MERCHANDISE RETURNS

SYMPTOMS

- Customer complaints.
- Loss of customers.
- Returned delivery charges paid by the seller.
- Government investigation for consumer fraud.
- Having to give customers incentives to keep merchandise.

CAUSES

- Poor quality merchandise.
- Incorrect or excessive pricing.
- Failure to meet specifications.

- Delivery problems.
- Deceptive advertising.

ANALYSIS

- Investigate the trend in the ratio of sales returns and allowances to sales. An increasing trend indicates customer dissatisfaction.
- Compare the original selling price and the final discounted selling price. Is the final price the result of competition, defects in the product, design obsolescence, or other problems?
- Prepare a returned-materials report for each transaction. A written report describing the materials and why they are being returned should accompany materials being put back into stock.

REPAIR

Encourage customers not to return goods:
- Offer sales discounts.
- Analyze and correct flaws in product quality.
- Provide free in-home service to correct problems.
- Improve packaging and shipping to minimize damage in delivery.
- Change an unreliable delivery service.
- Install an 800 telephone hot-line number for dissatisfied customers.
- Offer other free merchandise as a bonus.
- Give credits toward future purchases.
- Use new and unique styles.

Take immediate action on quality problems. Check quality at each phase of the production process rather than waiting until the finished product appears.

PREVENTION TECHNIQUES

Returns may be prevented by:
- Closely adhering to consumer laws.
- Implementing a total quality management (TQM) system.
- Using higher-quality materials and components for manufactured goods.
- Increasing inspection of goods before shipment.
- Improving billing procedures.

- Double-checking physical counts.
- Having legal staff check advertising.
- Dropping products with an above-average complaint and defect rate.
- Using public relations programs to promote the image of the company.
- Checking to ensure that products meet customer requirements.
- Surveying letters of complaint from dealers and customers.
- Testing new products for reliability and performance.
- Asking employees why products have quality problems.

SPILLOVER EFFECTS

- Declining sales and profits.
- Loss of future business.
- Criminal or civil lawsuits arising from product liability or false advertising.
- Consumer boycotts.
- A long-lasting negative reputation.

Chapter 12
Weak Internal Controls

A business with a weak internal control structure cannot survive. It will suffer losses from theft of assets, credit card fraud, and recordkeeping errors. The financial data it generates will be incorrect and unreliable, creating financial and legal problems. The company will enter into unauthorized transactions. It will suffer from operational inefficiencies and failure to follow prescribed managerial policies. The quality of its products or services and the efficiency of its employees will decline.

The financial problems addressed in this chapter are:
• Costs not closely tracked.
• Assets not monitored.
• Recordkeeping errors.
• Credit card fraud.
• Cumbersome accounting procedures.

PROBLEM
COSTS NOT CLOSELY TICKED
SYMPTOMS

• Critical documentation on costs to date does not exist or cannot be generated at the time it is needed.
• Expenses are above or below budget amounts.

- Checks are missing.
- Many expenses are charged to cash or to miscellaneous expense and not to specific accounts.
- Unusual or infrequent expenses are not recorded or are recorded incorrectly.
- The chart of accounts has been changed frequently to meet new reporting standards.
- Inventory and other assets are either overstated or understated.
- The ratio of gross profit to revenue is incorrectly calculated.
- Financial statements contain unreasonable expenditures or material omissions.
- Unauthorized individuals who have access to blank checks and a check-writing machine and are forging checks.
- Independent auditors discover fraud and embezzlement by individual employees.
- The company issues unnumbered checks that are not recorded in the accounting records.

CAUSES

- The accounting policy regarding documentation and recording of expenses is inadequate.
- Management is inexperienced or incompetent.
- Internal control procedures are inadequate.
- A single individual controls disbursements.
- Payments are made without authorization from higher authority.
- Internal controls for recording or disbursement of cash are inadequate or nonexistent.

ANALYSIS

Except for extraordinary items, companies have considerable leeway in classifying expenses, but generally accepted accounting principles (GAAP) do require that all items of profit and loss be recognized in the accounting period in which they occur. Expenses include accrual of estimated losses from loss contingencies. They are subject to budgetary controls, which can be very effective in highlighting deviations that require investigation. All expense items must be carefully recorded if net income is to be effective as a criterion for measuring current and estimating future performance.

REPAIR

- Evaluate internal control procedures for recording expenses.
- Examine expense balances.
- Analyze large unexplained variations in expense accounts from budgeted or prior-year amounts.
- Review all accounting procedures, operations, and ratio tests.
- Investigate substantial deviations from budgeted amounts.
- Number all authorizations for payments and checks.
- Evaluate the accounting staff and if necessary retrain them.
- Define lines of responsibility for recording expenses and disbursing cash.
- Review all liability transactions to ensure that all expenses have been recorded for the accounting period.

PREVENTION TECHNIQUES

- Establish internal control procedures for recording expenses.
- Design documentation to substantiate all cash disbursements.
- Set up a chart of accounts for each asset, liability, capital, income, and expense account.
- Ensure that the accounting staff is honest, competent, and trustworthy.
- Ensure that the check-writing machine is used only by authorized personnel.
- Require cosigners for large checks.

SPILLOVER EFFECTS

- Incorrect financial decisions.
- Auditor questions.
- Review by governmental agencies.
- Lawsuits for mismanagement and negligence.
- Declining prices for the company's stocks and bonds.
- A downgraded credit rating.
- Difficulty obtaining financing.

See also in this chapter: CUMBERSOME ACCOUNTING PROCEDURES *and* RECORDKEEPING ERRORS. *In Chapter 2:* CHECK FRAUD AND IMPROPER PAYMENTS. *In Chapter 6:* DISTORTED COST INFORMATION, INADEQUATE COST CONTROL.

PROBLEM
ASSETS NOT MONITORED
SYMPTOMS

- The company owns assets that are not recorded or that cannot be located.
- Physical assets, such as plant and equipment, are obsolete, damaged, or have no value.
- There is an abnormally high incidence of accounting errors related to classification of assets.
- The financial statement figures for assets are incorrect.
- Cash, inventory, and other assets are being stolen.
- The allowance for doubtful accounts is wrong, resulting in an unrealistic, unrealized accounts-receivable balance.
- Inaccurate depreciation and amortization methods have been applied to long-term assets.
- Goodwill, an intangible asset, is recorded on the books though there is no reasonable basis for it.

CAUSES

- Lack of physical safeguards and internal control over both current and long-lived assets.
- Technological innovations that make older assets, such as machinery and equipment, obsolete.
- Inaccurate accounting records.
- Failure to record asset purchases.
- Theft by dishonest employees and outsiders.
- Failure to keep valuable assets, such as securities, in a safe.

Failure to record and properly classify assets and expenses may be due to an incompetent accounting staff, a lack of internal controls, failure to keep up-to-date records, or use of incorrect accounting principles.

ANALYSIS

Business assets are separated into current assets and noncurrent assets, those that have a useful life of more than one year. Current assets (including cash, short-term investments, accounts receivable, and inventory) tend to be more liquid and are more prone to theft. The cost of long-lived assets (long-term investments, land, buildings, and equipment, intangible assets like patents and copyrights, and minerals in the ground) includes purchase price, transportation charges, brokerage commissions, legal fees, and back property taxes. Correct methods of depreciation, amortization, and depletion must be applied to long-term assets.

REPAIR

- Review the chart that classifies transactions into balance sheet and income statement accounts.
- Evaluate all internal control procedures.
- Conduct training programs on how to treat asset acquisitions.
- Where possible, put assets under lock and key.
- Investigate missing assets and file insurance claims to recover their cost.
- Examine vendor invoices and related documents to verify acquisition of equipment.
- If goodwill appears on the books, determine how it was calculated.

PREVENTION TECHNIQUES

- Implement in-house training programs to ensure that the accounting staff is honest, competent, and trustworthy.
- Make sure that there is adequate documentation of authorization for specific transactions.
- Safeguard physical assets and records. (For example, each physical asset should be given a serial number.)
- Establish independent checks on the accounting functions by both internal and external auditors.
- Inspect all assets bought and received by the company.
- Record the cost of assets constructed.
- Hold the employee in charge of specific assets responsible for shortages or other discrepancies.
- Change locks and security codes periodically.

SPILLOVER EFFECTS

If an accounting system and the accompanying internal control procedures are inadequate or inefficient, they will not generate reliable information about assets. As a result, the financial position and operating results of the company will be misstated. This will lead to incorrect financial decisions, audits, a decline in stock prices, reluctance by creditors to extend credit, and stockholder lawsuits.

See also in this chapter: COSTS NOT CLOSELY TRACKED, RECORDKEEPING ERRORS, *and* CUMBERSOME ACCOUNTING PROCEDURES. *In Chapter 3*: THEFT, MISCOUNTED INVENTORY, *and* INACCURATE INVENTORY RECORDS.

PROBLEM
RECORDKEEPING ERRORS

SYMPTOMS

- Misstatements on the financial statement.
- Restatement of previously prepared financial statements.
- Extension of the audit report due date.
- Incomplete records.
- Duplication of effort.
- Unproductive recordkeeping time.
- Disclosure of employee fraud and embezzlement.
- An increase in audit fees.
- A constant turnover of outside auditors because of disagreements.

CAUSES

- Incompetent or inexperienced accounting staff.
- Lack of internal controls.
- Absence of internal and external audits.
- Deficient organizational structure.
- Failure to assign responsibility among employees.
- Lack of up-to-date records.
- Use of incorrect accounting principles.

ANALYSIS

- Analyze the effect of recordkeeping errors on the financial statements.
- Determine the dollar amount of any theft and embezzlement.

- Evaluate failures to meet deadlines in accumulating and reporting financial information.
- Determine the ratio of audit fees to sales. A high ratio indicates that more audit time was required because of problems with the records or internal control procedures.

REPAIR

- Undertake internal and external audits to confirm financial statement figures.
- Prepare a monthly bank reconciliation to prove that the balance on the books reconciles with the balance at the bank.
- Periodically count major assets, such as inventory and long-term assets.
- Correct errors immediately.
- Ask an independent CPA firm to evaluate the accounting system and make written recommendations for improvement.
- Use computerized accounting software to improve accuracy and timeliness.
- Use the Sarbanes-Oxley Act compliance guidelines.
- Use audit and tax preparation software programs.

PREVENTION TECHNIQUES

- Ensure that the accounting staff is honest, competent, and trustworthy.
- Separate duties to ensure proper internal control.
- Make sure that procedures are properly authorized and documented.
- Safeguard physical assets and records.
- Establish an independent check on the accounting functions by both internal and external auditors.
- Set up an audit committee to review all audit procedures.

SPILLOVER EFFECTS

- Lack of reliable accounting information.
- Stockholder lawsuits.
- Drop in the market value of equity shares.
- Excessive loan restrictions.

• IRS disallowance of certain expenditures.

• Incorrect financial management decisions.

• Increased borrowing costs.

• Decline in the value of the company's shares.

• Difficulty issuing credit instruments.

See also in this chapter: CUMBERSOME ACCOUNTING PROCEDURES. *In Chapter 2*: CHECK FRAUD AND IMPROPER PAYMENTS.

PROBLEM
CREDIT CARD FRAUD

SYMPTOM

Unauthorized use of stolen or lost credit cards.

CAUSES

• Failure by employees to verify that the holder of the card is authorized to use it.

• Failure of a bank to cancel a card when there has been a report of fraudulent charges on it.

• Outdated information regarding lost or stolen credit cards.

• Employee fraud.

ANALYSIS

Credit cards offer consumers the convenience of buying goods without having to pay cash immediately. Retailers benefit because they do not have to check each customer's credit rating. However, credit card fraud is an inherent part of doing business. Millions of credit cards are in circulation today. A small percentage of them are lost or stolen annually, resulting in their unauthorized use by unscrupulous individuals.

REPAIR

• Train employees to verify that the person who presents a card for payment of a purchase is its true owner and is authorized to use it.

• Allow only specific employees to handle credit card purchases.

PREVENTION TECHNIQUES

- Check all credit card numbers for lost or stolen cards.
- Check the card's expiration date and the signature of the authorized user.
- Ask that the user show additional identification.
- Bond all employees who handle credit card transactions.
- Keep a file on all customers who have been known to participate in fraudulent transactions involving credit cards.

SPILLOVER EFFECTS

In the process of installing procedures to guard against credit card fraud, financial management should also evaluate the company's contract for credit card processing services. Because of competition in the industry, prices for these services have dropped sharply and improved options have proliferated.

PROBLEM
CUMBERSOME ACCOUNTING PROCEDURES

SYMPTOMS

- No ease of use.
- Net losses.
- Abnormally high incidence of errors.
- Misstated financial statement figures.
- Restatement of previously prepared financial statements.
- Extension of the audit report due date.
- Generation of large amounts of unimportant information.
- Incomplete records.
- Failure to disclose information.
- Duplication of effort.
- Unproductive use of time.
- Theft of cash, inventory, and other assets.
- Disclosure of employee fraud and embezzlement.
- An expensive increase in the amount of time outside auditors must spend going over accounts.
- Constant turnover in outside auditors because of disagreements.

CAUSES

- Incompetent or inexperienced accounting staff.
- Lack of internal controls.
- Absence of internal and external audits.
- Deficient organizational structure.
- Failure to keep records current.
- Use of incorrect accounting principles.

ANALYSIS

- Analyze recordkeeping errors and their effect on the financial statements.
- Determine the dollar amount of any theft and embezzlement sustained.
- Analyze reasons for failure to meet deadlines in accumulating and reporting financial information.
- Evaluate the ratio of audit fees to sales. A high ratio indicates that more audit time was required because of problems with the accounting records.

REPAIR

- Ensure that internal controls are sufficient to safeguard assets.
- Immediately correct any accounting errors discovered.

PREVENTION TECHNIQUES

- Implement in-house training programs to assure that the accounting staff' is current on the latest pronouncements of the American Institute of CPAs, the Financial Accounting Standards Board, and the IRS.
- Replace outdated systems.
- Streamline the process for documenting transactions.

SPILLOVER EFFECTS

If an accounting system is inadequate, it will not generate reliable information. As a result, the company's financial position and operating results may be misstated. This will lead to audits and to disallowances by governmental agencies. Creditors may also sue. Loan restrictions will be more stringent. There may be stockholder derivative suits.

*See also in this chapter:*RECORDKEEPING ERRORS.

Chapter 13
Business Ownership Threatened

If a company cannot meet its impending obligations, it will become insolvent and possibly go bankrupt. Indications of looming problems are operating losses, cash deficiencies, failure to obtain credit, a sudden drop in the prices of a firm's securities, and inability to realize cash from assets.

Management can take many steps to protect itself against business failure. Avoid excessive debt, stagger debt payments, lengthen the maturity dates of debt, match the maturity dates of debt with the maturity dates of assets (hedging), sell off unprofitable business segments and low-return assets, obtain adequate insurance, diversify horizontally and vertically, avoid markets on the downturn or those that are highly competitive, and not overextend itself either financially or operationally.

Another threat is hostile takeover by another firm. Such a takeover may lead to increased costs, lack of financial synergies, and employee resentment.

The following financial problems are covered in this chapter:
- Bankruptcy on the Horizon.
- Inability to curb financial problems.
- Inability to repay debt.
- Takeover threat.

• Increased costs after acquisition.

• Financial inconsistencies after acquisition.

PROBLEM
BANKRUPTCY ON THE HORIZON

SYMPTOMS

• Declining profitability or increasing losses.

• Cash flow inadequacies.

• Inability to pay liabilities on their due dates.

• Financing unavailable.

• Outside auditors withdrawal from the engagement.

• Contraction in the business.

• Cessation of dividends.

• Violation of loan agreements.

• Lawsuits.

• Criminal and civil charges.

• Sharp decline in credit rating.

• Significant decline in the price of company stocks and bonds.

• Increased business risk.

CAUSES

• Deficient financial health.

• Poor financial planning and management.

• Lack of financial goals and objectives.

• Lawsuits.

• Product line deficiencies.

• Unethical conduct.

• Poor relationship with creditors and investors.

• Inadequate insurance against losses.

• Lack of cash.

• Too much leverage.

• Inability to raise money due to poor credit rating.

• Incompetent professional management.

• Damages and costs paid in litigation.

• Bad reputation of the firm resulting from criminal as well as civil penalties (as in the case of product liability).

ANALYSIS

A study done by W. Beaver1 found that bankruptcy could be predicted at least five years before it happened by looking at certain ratios—the most important being cash flow to total debt, net income to total assets, and total debt to total assets. Beaver's cash flow ratio (net income plus depreciation divided by total debt) predicts bankruptcy within the next two years if the ratio is less than 1.

E. Altman[2] formulated a mathematical model, the Z-score, that can also be used to predict bankruptcy within the short run (one or two years). The Z-score equals:

$$\frac{\text{Working capital}}{\text{Total assets}} \times 1.2 + \frac{\text{Retained earnings}}{\text{Total assets}} \times 1.4 + \frac{\text{Operating income}}{\text{Total assets}} \times 3.3$$

$$+ \frac{\text{Market value of common stock and preferred stock (or net worth for private companies)}}{\text{Total debt}}$$

$$\times 0 \, 6 + \frac{\text{Sales}}{\text{Total assets}} \times 1.$$

Altman's scoring chart is shown in Table 13.1.

TABLE 13.1. THE ALTMAN BANKRUPTCY PREDICTION CHART

Score	Probability of Short-Term Illiq
1.80 or less	Very high
1.81 to 2.7	High
2.8 to 2.9	Possible
3.0 or higher	Not likely

The score is important for management because it suggests when capital expansion and dividends should be curtailed to keep needed funds within the business.

---

[1]Beaver, W. "Financial Ratios as Predictors of Failure." *Empirical Research in Accounting: Selected Studies* (1966), Supplement to *Journal of Accounting Research.* 4:77-111

[2]Altman, E. "Financial Ratios, Discriminant Analysis and the Prediction for Corporate Bankruptcy." *Journal of Finance.* September 1978, 589-609.

Example: Company H provides the following data.

Working capital	$250,000
Total assets	900,000
Total liabilities	300,000
Retained earnings	200,000
Sales	1,000,000
Operating income	150,000
Common stock	
Book value	210,000
Market value	300,000
Preferred stock	
Book value	100,000
Market value	160,000

The Z-score is:

$$\frac{\$250,000}{\$900,000} \times 1.2 + \frac{\$200,000}{\$900,000} \times 1.4 + \frac{\$150,000}{\$900,000} \times 3.3 + \frac{\$460,000}{\$300,00} \times 0.6 + \frac{\$1,000,000}{\$900,000} \times 1$$

$$=0.333+0.312+0.550+0.920+1.11=3.225.$$

The probability that Company H will fail is very low.

E. Altman, R. Haldeman, and P. Narayanan[3] uncovered the following eight measures as best for forecasting bankruptcy (1) operating income to total assets, (2) earnings stability, (3) times-interest-earned, (4) retained earnings to total assets, (5) current ratio, (7) common equity to total capital, and (8) total assets.

For a fee, ZETA Services will determine the possibility of business failure within five years using the company's ZETA model.

REPAIR

- Lengthen the maturity dates of debt and modify interest rates.
- Sell off unprofitable business segments and low-return assets.
- Restrict capital expansion during economic downturns.
- Reduce prices on slow-moving inventory.

---

[3]Altman, E., R. Haldeman, and P. Narayanan. "ZETA Analysis: A New Model to Identify Bankruptcy Risk of Corporations." *Journal of Banking and Finance*. October 1977, 29-54.

PREVENTION TECHNIQUES

- Avoid excessive debt and stagger debt payments.
- Anticipate future trends in the marketplace.
- Assure that insurance coverage is adequate.
- Be careful about going from a labor-intensive to a capital-intensive situation when the economy looks dismal.
- Make expenditures for future growth, such as research and development.
- Avoid operations in risky areas.
- Emphasize the hedging approach to finance by matching the due dates on debt to the maturity dates of assets.
- Keep current on changes in technology.
- Diversify horizontally and vertically.
- Avoid moving into industries with a history of failure.
- Avoid long-term fixed-fee contracts.
- Avoid markets on the downturn or those that are very competitive.
- Do not overextend financially or operationally.
- Manage assets, such as cash, receivables, and inventory, to receive attractive returns while controlling risk.

SPILLOVER EFFECTS

- Lawsuits for damages caused to creditors and investors because of poor financial management.
- Termination of financial managers and other employees.
- Legal costs and other administrative expenses incurred in the process of liquidating or reorganizing the company.

See in Chapter 5: EXCESSIVE DEBT, INADEQUATE LIQUIDITY, *and* INSOLVENCY.

PROBLEM
INABILITY TO CURB
FINANCIAL PROBLEMS

SYMPTOMS

- A company makes radical policy changes too quickly.
- Decisions are based on intuition rather than on detailed research about market conditions.

- Critical daily problems are not resolved.
- The company has not had a significant product or service success in years and is considered a follower rather than a leader in its industry.
- The company is not keeping up with market, technological, and industry trends.
- The firm continues to lose money after developing products and fails to establish a foothold in the market.
- Targeted production goals and quotas are not met, are late, or are over budget.
- While diversifying to reduce risk, the organization is doing nothing for its shareholders.
- Creditors are not being paid.
- There are union grievances by employees claiming unfair treatment.
- There is high employee turnover.
- Customers complain about the poor quality of the company's services and products.
- There is excessive return of products and recalls for faulty manufacture or design.
- Publicity is negative.
- The firm is only marginally profitable and suffers from cash flow problems and declining sales.
- Dividends are paid from borrowed funds.
- Financial statements are erroneous or fraudulent and there is waste and theft of assets. The annual report is delayed.
- Accounting practices are questionable.
- Executives are taking excessive compensation payments and fringe benefits during a period of low earnings.

CAUSES

- Failure to develop new products.
- Failure to preserve major historical markets.
- Deterioration in operational efficiency.
- Unproductive diversification.
- Poor-quality products.
- Questionable financial policies.

- Resources diverted to new ventures where management lacks expertise.
- Unstable management due to high turnover.
- Lack of managerial experience.
- Lack of cooperation between management and labor.
- Lack of ethics and ideals.
- Poor example set by upper management.
- Workers pressed for concessions, without any concessions from management.
- Variable costs exceeding variable revenue.
- Highly technical products that break down frequently.

ANALYSIS

- Examine the trend in units produced relative to industry units produced, and analyze company revenue as a percent of total industry revenue.
- Examine the trends in profit margin, operating expenses to revenue, manufacturing cost to revenue, and inventory turnover.
- Examine the extent to which cost changes relate to changes in sales.
- Compare company costs to those of other companies in the industry.

REPAIR

- Improve operational effectiveness.
- Create highly differentiated products at low cost.
- Retire or terminate unproductive employees.
- Put financial management personnel in control of expenditures.
- Conduct studies to determine what customers are buying.
- Ensure that the company builds a reputation for integrity and fairness.
- Focus on fewer products of higher quality.
- Restructure to divest the firm of marginal or unprofitable branches, divisions, and subsidiaries.
- Eliminate excesses in parts of the organization.
- Use as a rule of thumb, no more than four top-level officers per $1 billion in sales.

- Form committees to study each of the company's problem areas. The compensation committee could review the benefits package given to key employees, for example, while a sales committee could evaluate the advertising program.
- Retain earnings and establish new lines of credit.
- Review the dividend policy. Dividend payments may be too high relative to the company's limited profit prospects.
- Restrict dividend payments.
- Consider selling common stock to generate funds for acquiring a company with a proven earnings record (with the caveat that too much diversification may put the company back into financial instability).
- Redesign products to lower manufacturing costs.
- Review the production facilities and replace or retool machinery that has a record of malfunctioning.

PREVENTION TECHNIQUES

- Send experienced financial troubleshooting teams to different divisions, departments, and subsidiaries to solve problems.
- Clearly state the company's policies and production goals.
- Make financial decisions only after all information has been accumulated from several independent sources that can confirm its accuracy.
- Protect established markets before attempting to enter new ones.
- Become a low-cost provider of distinguished products and services.
- Standardize production parts.
- Invest in facilities that produce only profitable items that are in demand.
- Improve the technical abilities of current financial management.
- Offer early retirement to older, less competent managers. Hire people with a proven record of success.
- Attempt to renegotiate prices with suppliers or seek cheaper alternate sources of supply.

SPILLOVER EFFECTS

If financial managers cannot alter the operating policy of the company, it may fail and seek bankruptcy or reorganization protection.

See also in this chapter: BANKRUPTCY ON THE HORIZON. *In Chapter 5:* INADEQUATE LIQUIDITY *and* INSOLVENCY.[4]

PROBLEM
INABILITY TO REPAY DEBT

SYMPTOMS

- The business is short on cash inflows.
- It has difficulty obtaining financing.
- It has difficulty collecting notes and accounts receivable, converting short-term investments into cash, and obtaining credit from suppliers.
- It cannot buy inventory or assets, has low profitability, and cannot take cash discounts by making early payment.
- Its credit rating is deteriorating.
- Fixed interest costs are high, and debt is excessive.

CAUSES

- Inability to obtain funds to finance expansion.
- Poor operating performance, coupled with deficient cash flow.
- Liabilities in excess of the company's ability to pay.
- Additional debt incurred in an attempt to prevent a hostile takeover by another company.
- Management incompetence.

ANALYSIS

There are many measures to appraise a company's ability to repay debt. *See* INADEQUATE LIQUIDITY *and* INSOLVENCY *in Chapter 5* for full coverage of them.

---

[4]For an informative discussion of this topic, see Frederick Zimmerman. The Turnaround Experience: Real World Lessons in Revitalizing Corporations. 1991. New York: McGrawHill.

REPAIR

- Reduce company expansion or obtain additional financing.
- Sell assets.
- Change the amount and timing of future cash flows in preparation for unexpected developments.
- Offer creditors stock in place of cash repayment of debt.

PREVENTION TECHNIQUES

- Better planning for acquisition of capital facilities.
- Reduced expansion efforts.
- Securing new lines of credit.
- Synchronizing cash outlays to cash inflows.
- Modifying the budgeting process to improve forecasts of demand for capital expenditures so that funds are available to repay debt.
- Improved financial planning to anticipate future conditions in the economy and money market.
- Using hedging in financing by matching the maturity dates of debt to the collection date or maturity date of assets.

SPILLOVER EFFECTS

A poor working capital position means that the company is less liquid. Inadequate liquidity will result in lower credit ratings, decline in the market price of the company's stocks and bonds, higher interest rates on borrowings, unavailability of financing, financial inability to make profitable investments at the right time, and, in severe cases, insolvency and bankruptcy.

If debts cannot be repaid, there will be increased cost of capital, higher compensating balances, increased business risk, higher financing costs, and financial instability. A business may fail if it cannot obtain credit to meet its financial obligations.

A company that is out of cash cannot operate effectively and its profitability will decline and ultimately disappear.

See also in this chapter: BANKRUPTCY ON THE HORIZON. *In Chapter 1:* INADEQUATE CASH POSITION *and* CASH OUTFLOWS EXCEEDING CASH INFLOWS. *In Chapter 5:* INADEQUATE LIQUIDITY, EXCESSIVE DEBT, INADEQUATE WORKING

CAPITAL, INSOLVENCY, *and* POOR PROFITABILITY AND GROWTH. *In Chapter 7*: INABILITY TO OBTAIN FINANCING.

PROBLEM
TAKEOVER THREAT
SYMPTOMS

- The market value of the common stock is below its book value.
- The company has incurred continuous operating losses and has a tax-loss carry-forward that makes it an attractive takeover candidate.
- The company is cash-rich and has significant growth potential or a low debt/equity ratio.

CAUSES

A purchaser, or a raider, seeks to acquire another company for one of several reasons:

- The target company may own highly liquid assets, have a high rate of return, own one or more successful products, have successful management and sales teams, have a reputation for reliability and integrity, offer research capability, or have profitable sales territories that the acquiring company seeks to penetrate.
- The purchaser may be seeking to eliminate competition by acquiring a competitor.
- The purchaser wants to diversify its operations.
- The purchaser may be pursuing a policy of external growth over internal growth. External growth might be the best solution if the target company has low-cost assets, greater economy of scale, a better and more secure supply of raw materials, a reliable source of labor and managerial skills, the possibility for rapid growth, and the opportunity to diversify the purchaser's product line.
- The purchaser may be seeking to offset the operating losses of the target company against its own profits to achieve considerable tax savings.
- The purchaser is trying to smooth out the cyclical movement of its earnings.

ANALYSIS

The term *business combination* refers to any situation in which two or more organizations are joined together in common ownership. Business combinations can be accomplished in various ways. First, a company can acquire the assets, and possibly the liabilities, of the target company in exchange for cash and stock. In an alternative approach, a company can acquire the stock of the target company in exchange for cash and stock. In yet another gambit, a company can achieve legal control over another company simply by acquiring a majority of its voting stock.

After a takeover, the acquiring company has control of the target company and may either retain it as a separate legal entity or dissolve it and merge the activities of the two companies. If the acquired company continues to function, it must maintain its own corporate officers, board of directors, and independent accounting system. The acquiring company may elect to file consolidated tax returns if it makes certain tax elections available under the Internal Revenue Code, so that any operating losses generated by one company can be offset against the profits of the other.

REPAIR

Current business strategy emphasizes continuous expansion of major corporations. To avoid an unfriendly takeover by a raider, management might turn to one or more of the antitakeover measures called shark repellents:

- *Rescue by a white knight.* In this move, the target company is "saved" by a third, "friendly" company that is willing to enter into a bidding war against the raider.
- *The Pacman defense.* The target company makes a takeover bid of its own for the stock of the company attempting to take it over.
- *A poison pill.* The target company makes its acquisition more expensive for the raider by enacting a provision (the "poison pill") that lets current shareholders buy additional shares at a price well below market value.
- *Greenmail.* In what is essentially an effort to buy off the raider, the target of the takeover enters into a transaction whereby it pays the raider a premium ("greenmail") well over the market price to buy its shares back.

PREVENTION TECHNIQUES

- Stagger the terms of the board of directors over several years, so that the entire board of directors does not come up for election all at once. A potential raider will thus have difficulty gaining control by electing its own board of directors.
- Amend the corporate charter to require that a super majority of voting shares be required to approve any takeover proposals.
- Sue to delay a takeover and make it more expensive and thus less attractive to the raider.

SPILLOVER EFFECTS

Acquiring another company in the same industry may trigger antitrust action. If the takeover bid is successful, the purchaser may also have to decide whether the acquisition is to be treated and accounted for as a pooling of interests or a purchase. An unsuccessful takeover may have a negative effect on earnings, due to inefficiencies in the combined unit.

See also in this chapter: INCREASED COSTS AFTER ACQUISITION *and* FINANCIAL INCONSISTENCIES AFTER ACQUISITION.

PROBLEM
INCREASED COSTS AFTER ACQUISITION

SYMPTOMS

- Operating costs are disproportionate to combined revenues.
- The expected synergistic effect on earnings does not materialize.
- EPS for both companies decrease.

CAUSES

- Acquisition of incompatible or obsolete assets.
- Duplicate production facilities.
- Adjustment of pay scales.
- Too many nonproductive employees.
- Costs of servicing acquisition debt.
- Higher insurance costs because of increased risks.
- Increased legal and accounting costs.
- Substantial residual costs from unsuccessful defense strategies.
- An outflow of valuable managerial talent.

ANALYSIS

A variety of preacquisition expenses may be incurred in consummating a corporate takeover. Costs of organizing a subsidiary to acquire the target corporation, start-up expenses of the new subsidiary, takeover defense expenses of the target corporation, and greenmail expenses of either the purchaser or the target corporation.

REPAIR

- After the acquisition, announce what the policy of the new management will be. This will reduce employee anxieties and public rumors that may adversely affect the market value of the purchaser's shares.
- Formulate consistent accounting procedures for both companies.
- Adopt similar tax policies.
- Write off obsolete inventory.
- Sell off or close duplicate production facilities and use the proceeds to retire debt.
- Terminate nonproductive and nonessential employees.
- Use the operating loss of the target company to reduce the purchaser's taxes.
- Examine the dividend policy of both companies. Continuity of dividend payments for both companies can reassure investors.
- Treat the acquisition as a pooling of interests. (Poolings require virtually no cash or new debt to complete.)

PREVENTION TECHNIQUES

- Adopt a uniform accounting policy for both companies to avoid misleading financial statements.
- Prepare consolidated financial statements to diminish risk and increase the P/E ratio even if potential earnings growth is unchanged.

SPILLOVER EFFECTS

- Labor problems.
- Negative publicity.
- Reduction in the market value of the purchaser's shares
- Payout of termination payments to discharged executives (golden parachutes).

• Legal costs.

See also in this chapter: FINANCIAL INCONSISTENCIES AFTER ACQUISITION *and* TAKEOVER THREAT.

PROBLEM
FINANCIAL INCONSISTENCIES AFTER ACQUISITION

SYMPTOMS

• Accounting principles and policies are inconsistent.
• Accounting estimates are unrealistic.
• Tax treatments of major transactions differ.
• The fiscal year-end for each company is different.
• Operating costs bear no relationship to revenues.
• The expected synergistic effect from the acquisition of another company does not materialize.

CAUSE

Inconsistent accounting treatment for revenue and expenses.

ANALYSIS

• Analyze the accounting policies of both companies and their effect on the financial statements.
• Investigate any cash flow problems.

REPAIR

• Make all accounting procedures consistent.
• Retrain the accounting staff.

PREVENTION TECHNIQUES

• Form an accounting committee to evaluate the advantages of alternative methods of accounting.
• Ensure that the accounting staff is current on the latest pronouncements of the AICPA, the Financial Accounting Standards Board, and the IRS.

SPILLOVER EFFECT

A financial picture that is misleading to creditors and investors.

See also in this chapter: INCREASED COSTS AFTER ACQUISITION _and_ TAKEOVER THREAT. _In Chapter 8:_ MANAGEMENT UNAWARE OF FINANCIAL PROBLEMS. _In Chapter 12:_ CUMBERSOME ACCOUNTING PROCEDURES.

Chapter 14
Tax Planning and Preparation

Tax avoidance is merely using legal and tax accounting techniques to minimize taxes paid. It is the proper objective of all tax planning. Inadequate or improper tax recordkeeping can result in misstated tax return data, placing the business in possible civil and criminal violation of the Internal Revenue Code. Underpayment of taxes can result in penalties, as well as in civil or criminal liability. Improper tax planning will usually cause a higher than normal tax burden that will lower profits.

In this chapter, we consider the following problems:

• Incomplete and inaccurate tax recordkeeping.

• Underpayment of estimated taxes.

• Double taxation.

• Incorrect classification of employees.

• Fringe benefits not recorded as income.

• Excessive compensation to employee shareholders.

• Funds insufficient to buy a deceased shareholder's stock.

PROBLEM
INCOMPLETE AND INACCURATE
TAX RECORDKEEPING

SYMPTOMS

- An abnormally high incidence of errors affecting the company's tax liability.
- Misstated financial statement figures.
- Lack of tax documentation.
- Ignorance of tax laws.
- Failure to define staff responsibilities for filing tax reports.
- Stockholder lawsuits charging that opportunities for large tax savings were lost.
- IRS and state imposition of additional taxes, interest, and penalties.
- Excessive professional fees paid to tax accountants and lawyers.

CAUSES

- Incompetent or inexperienced accounting staff.
- Lack of internal controls.
- Deficient organizational structure for tax reporting.
- Management failure to keep current with changes in the tax laws.
- Use of incorrect tax-accounting principles.

ANALYSIS

- Review the accuracy and appropriateness of tax recordkeeping.
- Analyze errors and their effect on the financial statements.
- Evaluate reasons for the company's inability to meet tax filing deadlines and failure to make favorable tax elections.

REPAIR

- Assign staff responsibility for tax accounting and filings.
- Ask an independent CPA firm to evaluate tax preparation software programs.
- Analyze the effect of conditions imposed on the company by the IRS.
- Hire competent tax accountants.

PREVENTION TECHNIQUE

Ensure that the accounting staff is current on tax law and procedures.

SPILLOVER EFFECTS

- Excessive nondeductible tax penalties and high interest charges.
- Charges of inept and negligent management and corporate waste.
- IRS audits.
- Stockholder derivative suits.

See also in this chapter: UNDERPAYMENT OF TAXES. *In Chapter 6*: LACK OF COST INFORMATION. *In Chapter 12*: RECORDKEEPING ERRORS *and* CUMBERSOME ACCOUNTING PROCEDURES.

PROBLEM
UNDERPAYMENT OF TAXES

SYMPTOMS

- Penalty statements from the IRS and state tax departments.
- Warnings from internal audit staff, outside independent auditors, or legal counsel that the enterprise is not making its quarterly estimated payments.

CAUSES

- Failure to define staff responsibilities.
- Ignorance of tax laws.
- Weak internal controls.
- Lack of operating cash.

ANALYSIS

To figure the correct estimated tax, the company must calculate its expected sales, other income (such as dividend and interest received from outside investments), expenses, taxable income, estimated tax liability, and available tax credits.

REPAIR

- Define staff responsibility for making estimated tax payments.
- Announce due dates of all estimated tax payments.

PREVENTION TECHNIQUES

- Train the accounting staff to recognize problems that affect the company's tax liability.
- Prepare a quarterly income statement calculating the amount of the quarterly estimated tax payment.

SPILLOVER EFFECTS

- Excessive nondeductible tax penalties and high interest charges.
- Charges of inept and negligent management.

PROBLEM
DOUBLE TAXATION

SYMPTOM

The corporation is paying tax at a rate of 15 to 34 percent, leaving less available to be distributed to shareholders as dividends. Any amount that is distributed as a dividend is again subject to taxation at the shareholder level.

CAUSE

Failure to elect S corporation status.

ANALYSIS

To avoid double taxation, elect S corporation status. To make the election, three shareholder requirements must be satisfied on each day of the tax year:

1. The corporation may not have more than 75 shareholders (a married couple counts as only one shareholder).
2. All shareholders must be individuals, estates, or certain kinds of trusts.
3. Shareholders cannot be nonresident aliens.

Election of S corporation status is valid only if all shareholders consent. The election to be treated as an S corporation can be made at any time during the tax year before the election year or on or before the 15th day of the third month of the election year. Form 2553 must be used. The corporation must have authorized and issued only one class of either voting or nonvoting common stock.

The S corporation rules were enacted to permit small corporations to enjoy the nontax advantages of corporations without being subject to double taxation. Once an S corporation is elected, the tax treatment is almost like that of partnership taxation, in that income and losses of the corporation flow through, under the conduit principle, directly to the shareholders.

REPAIR

Elect S corporation status.

PREVENTION TECHNIQUES

- Comply with the statutory requirements for S corporations.
- Monitor all transfers of S corporation stock to make sure that the transferee is not an ineligible shareholder.
- Establish procedures for buying the stock of deceased shareholders.
- Make sure, when selling stock, that the number of shareholders does not exceed 75.
- Monitor married stockholders. When a stockholder couple gets divorced, if they share the stock, they would now be two shareholders rather than one.
- If the S corporation was previously a C corporation or merges with a C corporation, all S corporation investment activities should be monitored to ensure that passive investment income limitations for S corporations are not violated. (Passive investment income generally consists of gross receipts from interest, dividends, rents, royalties, annuities, and gains from sales or exchanges of stock or securities.) If an S corporation has C corporation earnings and profits passive income in excess of 25 percent of its gross receipts for three consecutive years, the S election is terminated as of the beginning of the following tax year. Once an S corporation election is terminated, the company must usually wait five years before electing S corporation status again.

SPILLOVER EFFECTS

The structure of an S corporation can create hardships to shareholders who receive large amounts of income flowing through without actual distributions of cash with which to help pay the tax on the income. Election of S corporation status also means that a corporation cannot accumulate profit in the corporation with the intent of declaring a dividend at a later date, when shareholders may be in a lower tax bracket.

An S corporation cannot issue both common and preferred stock. The S corporation can, however, issue common stock with both voting and nonvoting rights without impairing the S corporation election. If the common stock has differences in distribution or liquidation rights, this will impair the S corporation election. This limitation on the capital structure will also prevent the S corporation from going public, unless it revokes the S election.

PROBLEM
INCORRECT CLASSIFICATION OF EMPLOYEES

SYMPTOMS

- Payroll costs are not being recorded.
- Tax agencies are constantly monitoring the company's records to investigate possible payroll violations.
- Union representatives claim that the employer is not adhering to the union contract regarding payments of vacation and fringe benefits.

CAUSES

- Management is treating some people who should be considered employees as independent contractors so that payroll taxes and employee benefits do not have to be paid. Unrecorded payroll costs result in erroneous product and expense costs.
- Company policy fails to differentiate between who is an independent contractor and who is an employee.

ANALYSIS

Hiring an outside auditor, attorney, or contractor to perform a function specifically entailing the use of professional skills is securing the services of an independent contractor. IRS regulations provide that physicians, lawyers, contractors, "and others who follow an independent trade, business, or profession, in which they offer their services to the public, are not employees."

Where the employer controls the quality of the performance and the hours of employment and provides the tools necessary to complete the assigned task, the person performing the work is properly classified as an employee subject to payroll taxes, federal and state unemployment insurance, workers compensation, and union and pension benefits.

Under the Internal Revenue Code, an employer is liable for the amounts that must be withheld from the wages of an employee. The code contains numerous civil penalties for diverse but sometimes overlapping delinquencies, such as failure to file, negligence, and fraud.

REPAIR

- Study the definitions in federal, state, and local laws to understand who is an employee and who may be properly classified as an independent contractor.
- Review old payroll audits to learn how management classified the employment status of persons performing work for the company.

PREVENTION TECHNIQUES

- When hiring new employees, have them fill out a complete employment record, including their name, address, Social Security number, past employment history, and education and the company function for which they were hired.
- Have internal and external accountants review all service contracts and employment forms to determine whether an individual is correctly classified as an independent contractor or an employee.
- Request a ruling from the Internal Revenue Service if the status of a new employee is unclear.
- Train accounting and personnel staff in proper classification of new employees.

SPILLOVER EFFECTS

- Unrecorded payroll costs may lead to undervaluation of inventory and depreciable assets.
- Interest and penalties may be levied for failure to pay payroll taxes.
- Stockholder lawsuits may ensue.
- Expensive payroll tax audits may be necessary to assist outside government and union auditors.

PROBLEM
FRINGE BENEFITS NOT RECORDED AS INCOME

SYMPTOMS

- Penalty statements from the IRS and state tax departments.
- Warnings from tax authorities or auditors that the company is failing to report certain fringe benefits as taxable income.
- Complaints from employees that they have been questioned by the IRS about whether they have received certain taxable company benefits that have not been reported on their personal tax returns.

CAUSES

- Failure to define staff responsibilities.
- Ignorance of tax laws.
- Weak internal control.
- Inexperienced staff.

ANALYSIS

When a fringe benefit is taxable, the amount includable in gross income generally equals the fair market value of the benefit, reduced by the amount, if any, paid by the employee for it. The cost to the employer is generally not relevant.

Certain fringe benefits are nontaxable if the employee receives services, not property; if the employer does not incur substantial cost; and if the services are offered to customers in the ordinary course of the business in which the employee works. These nontaxable employee benefits include:

- No-additional-cost services, such as allowing an airline employee to fly free.
- Qualified employee discounts.
- Working-condition fringe benefits, such as free use of a company parking space.
- *De minimis* fringe benefits, such as permitting a company secretary to type a personal letter.

REPAIR

- Review company records to determine who has use of company cars, has company-paid membership in country clubs, or received tickets to entertainment events.
- Specify in writing which employee benefits are taxable and which nontaxable.

PREVENTION TECHNIQUES

- Train accounting staff to recognize taxable benefits.
- Periodically review accounting records to determine which benefits, if any, are taxable.
- Have a stated policy for valuing taxable fringe benefits.

SPILLOVER EFFECTS

- Excessive nondeductible tax penalties and high interest charges.
- Audits of the personal tax returns of employees who received taxable fringe benefits but did not report them.

PROBLEM
EXCESSIVE COMPENSATION TO EMPLOYEE SHAREHOLDERS

SYMPTOMS

- Salaries in excess of those ordinarily paid for similar services.
- Payments bearing a close relationship to the stockholdings of officers.

CAUSE

Management desires to distribute a dividend to employee-shareholders in the form of lower taxed salary payments.

ANALYSIS

Among the ordinary and necessary expenses of carrying on any trade or business is reasonable compensation for personal services actually rendered to the corporation by an employee who is also a shareholder. The employee is usually a corporate officer. The test of deductibility is whether the compensation is in fact payment purely for services rendered to the corporation. If it is determined that the amount of compensation is disproportionate, it is not deductible by the corporation and will be treated by the IRS as distribution of a dividend.

There is no precise rule to determine the exact amount of compensation that is reasonable. It may be assumed that it is the amount that would ordinarily be paid for like services by similar enterprises under similar circumstances. The circumstances to be considered are those existing when the contract for services was made, not when the contract is questioned by the IRS.

Failure of a closely-held corporation to pay dividends is a very significant factor in the IRS determination of whether the compensation deduction is allowable. If the payments for compensation bear a close relationship to stockholdings and are found to be distributions of earnings or profits, excessive payments will be nondeductible.

The IRS is particularly interested in situations where an employee with a controlling interest in a corporation receives an especially large compensation, especially where the corporation has a history of paying small dividends.

REPAIR

- The corporation must be prepared to show the IRS that the compensation was ordinary and necessary in carrying on the business.
- It must also show that the payments represent the purchase price for services rendered to the corporation and that the amount is fair and reasonable.

PREVENTION TECHNIQUES

- Prepare a checklist of factors used to determine compensation for the employee, including:
  - The employee's qualifications.
  - Number of persons available who are capable of performing the same duties.
  - Nature and extent of the employee's work.
  - Size and complexity of the business.
  - Profitability of the corporation.
  - Prevailing economic conditions.
  - A comparison of salaries with dividend distributions to shareholders.
  - Amount of compensation paid to the employee in previous years.
- The employee-shareholder can enter into a hedge agreement with the corporation stating that in case any portion of the salary paid is disallowed by the IRS the employee will refund the excess amount to the corporation.

SPILLOVER EFFECTS

- Continuing attention from the IRS.
- Inclusion of excessive payments for compensation for personal services in the gross income of the recipient.

PROBLEM
FUNDS INSUFFICIENT TO BUY A DECEASED SHAREHOLDER'S STOCK

SYMPTOM

When a shareholder dies, the corporation is not able to buy that person's stock as it is required by prior agreement to do (or as it wants to do so that the shares are not sold to strangers or vulnerable to purchase by a hostile group).

CAUSES

- Lack of adequate cash flow or cash on hand.
- Litigation preventing acquisition of stock.

ANALYSIS

The most significant disadvantage of the shareholder stock repurchase plan is that the corporation may lack the necessary funds.

REPAIR

- Borrow money to buy out the shareholder's heirs, using the shares as collateral.
- Buy life insurance, purchased by and payable to the corporation, to fund the corporation's repurchase obligation upon the deaths of future shareholders.

PREVENTION TECHNIQUES

Buy life insurance on all major stockholders whose deaths might trigger a repurchase agreement. The parties will sometimes want to take insurance proceeds into account in determining the price to be paid for a decedent's stock, based on a principle of fairness. If the insurance pays a corporation $100,000 as the result of a shareholder's death, and the corporation pays only $10,000 for the book value of the stock, the remaining shareholders will share the other $90,000, with none going to the heirs. If, on the other hand, the increased value of the corporation is used as the basis for evaluating the purchase price, the decedent's estate will receive the fair market value of the stock without giving the other shareholders an unintended windfall.

In setting up insurance in connection with a death redemption agreement, the corporation should be careful to be recognized as both the owner and the beneficiary of the policy.

SPILLOVER EFFECTS

The Internal Revenue Service may argue that the premiums paid by the corporation were taxable income to the insured shareholder because the shareholder is the real or beneficial owner of the insurance policy.

Glossary

Absorption (full) costing The complete cost of a product. The full unit manufacturing cost, consisting of direct materials, direct labor, and factory overhead.

Beta A measure of the company's risk relative to the market. It is the variation in the price of the stock relative to the variation in a stock market index (e.g., the Standard and Poor's 500). A beta of less than 1 means that the stock is less risky than the market.

Breakeven point The sales volume at which total revenue equals total cost, resulting in zero loss or profit.

Capital Asset Pricing Model (CAPM) A method of demonstrating the relationship between an investment's expected or required return and its beta.

Capital gain (loss) Appreciation (depreciation) in the market value of a stock.

CAPM. See Capital Asset Pricing Model.

Cash earnings Cash revenue less cash expenses. This is net income backed up by cash flow from operations.

Compensating balance A deposit that a bank requires that it can use to offset an unpaid loan. Because no interest is earned on the compensating balance, which is stated as a percentage of the loan, it increases the effective interest rate on the loan.

Contribution margin Sales less variable costs.

Correlation The relationship between variables, such as cost and volume. Correlation analysis evaluates cause-effect relationships. It looks consistently at how the value of one variable changes when the value of the other is changed. An example is the effect of advertising on sales.

Cost-volume-profit (CVP) The dollar impact a change in production volume has on costs and profit.

Current income Income received at stated periods, including interest, dividends, and rent.

CVP. See Cost-volume-profit.

Economic order quantity The optimum amount to order each time to minimize total inventory costs.

EFT. See Electronic funds transfer.

Elasticity The effect of a change in selling price on product demand.

Electronic funds transfer (EFT) A method of transferring funds using systems that are electronically linked via a communications network. Funds may be automatically transferred by telephone, telex, computer terminal, or microcomputer.

Exponential smoothing A weighted average of past data used as the basis for an estimate. This mathematical technique gives heaviest weight to more recent information and less weight to observations in the more distant past.

Financial leverage A measure of the financial risk that arises from fixed financial costs.

Financial model A system of mathematical equations, logic, and data that describes the relationship among financial and operating variables.

Flexible budget A budget that lists estimates at different capacity levels.

Float The time between the moment checks are deposited in a bank and the moment the depositor receives payment on them. Due to this time difference, many companies play the float by writing checks against money not presently in the account.

Holding period The time over which an investment is held.

Holding period return (HPR) The total return earned from holding an investment for a stated period.

HPR. See Holding period return.

Index number A ratio of a current year amount to a base (typical) year amount.

Insolvency A company's inability to pay debt.

JIT. See Just-in-time.

Just-in-time (JIT) An inventory management system in which the company buys and manufactures in small quantities just in time for use, thus minimizing inventory costs.

Lead time The number of days between placing an order and receiving delivery.

Liquidity Cash or assets readily convertible into cash.

Lockbox A box in a U. S. Postal Service facility used to facilitate collection of customer remittances. Use of a lockbox reduces processing float. The recipient's local bank empties the lockbox and deposits the funds periodically during the day.

Net monetary position Monetary assets less monetary liabilities.

Operating cycle The number of days from cash to inventory to accounts receivable to cash.

Operating leverage A measure of operating risk that arises from fixed operating costs.

PAC. See Pre-authorized check.

PAD. See Pre-authorized debit.

Payment draft A draft given to the bank for collection and then sent in turn to the issuer for acceptance. It allows for inspection of goods before payment.

Percentage of sales method A financial forecasting tool that estimates expenses for a future period as a percentage of the sales forecast.

Pre-authorized check (PAC) A check written by the payee on the payor's account and deposited on an agreed date.

Pre-authorized debit (PAD) Authorization given by the customer to the seller to automatically charge the customer's account.

Profit margin The ratio of net income to sales.

Raider A company attempting to acquire the assets or the stock of a target company that is unwilling to be acquired.

Recession A downturn in the economy. Many economists consider it a recession when there has been a decline in the gross national product for two consecutive quarters

Reorder point The inventory level at which it is appropriate to replenish stock.

Residual income Net income less minimum return on total assets.

Restructuring The reorganization of a company to reduce costs and improve efficiency.

Return on investment The ratio of net profit after taxes divided by total assets (invested capital).

Risk The chance of losing money.

Safety stock The amount of extra units of inventory carried as protection against possible stockouts.

Segmental reporting The presentation of financial information, such as profitability, by a major business segment, which may be product, major customer, division, department, or responsibility centers within a department.

Segment margin Contribution margin less direct (traceable) fixed costs.

Standard cost A predetermined cost that serves as a target.

Standard deviation A measure of the variability between actual and expected.

Static budget The budgeted costs at one capacity level only.

Sunk cost A past cost that is not affected by a current or future decision.

Total leverage A measure of total risk that refers to how earnings per share are affected by a change in sales. It equals the percentage change in EPS divided by the percentage change in sales. Total leverage at a given level of sales is the operating leverage multiplied by the financial leverage.

Total quality management (TQM) The use of high-quality materials, components, and labor in the manufacturing process.

TQM. See Total quality management.

Transfer price The price charged between divisions for internal transfer of an assembled product or service.

Variance The difference between actual and standard cost or revenue.

Venture capital A financing source for new businesses or turnaround ventures that combine much risk with potential for high return.

Working capital Current assets less current liabilities.

Alphabetical Index of Problems

About TEXERE

Texere, a progressive and authoritative voice in business publishing, brings to the global business community the expertise and insights of leading thinkers. Our books educate, enlighten, and entertain, and provide an intersection where our authors and our readers share cutting edge ideas, practices, and innovative solutions. Texere seeks to cultivate, enhance, and disseminate information that illuminates the global business landscape.

www.thomson.com/learning/texere

About the Typeface

This book was set in 11.5 point Times Roman. In 1931, The Times of London commissioned a new type design for the body copy of the paper. The design process was supervised by Stanley Morison. Times is actually a modernised version of the older typeface "Plantin", which Morison was instructed to use as the main basis for his new designs. Times font became the workhorse of the publishing industry and continues to be very popular, particularly for newspapers, magazines, and corporate communications such as proposals and annual reports. Due to its versatility, it remains a must-have typeface for today's designer.

Library of Congress Cataloging-in-Publication Data

Shim, Jae K.
  The financial troubleshooter : spotting and solving financial problems in your company / Jae K. Shim.
    p. cm.
  Rev. ed. of: The financial troubleshooter / Joel G. Siegel, Jae K. Shim, David Minars.
  Includes index.
  ISBN 0-324-20648-8 (hardcover : alk. paper)
  1. Corporations--Finance. I. Siegel, Joel G. Financial troubleshooter. II. Title.

  HG4026.S487 2005
  658.15--dc22

                          2005006820